The

RIDE

of a

LIFETIME

STORIES FROM AN UBER DRIVER

TOMMY FULTON

This book is dedicated to:

The Little Sisters of the Poor at Sacred Heart Residence in Mobile, Alabama, and the Men of St. Joseph at St. Dominic Parish in Mobile, Alabama.

Both taught me the power of prayer, and I am eternally grateful.

ACKNOWLEDGMENTS

I'm supposed to thank my family and friends in this section who are close to me and have been supportive and helpful. I will do so next. But first, I'm grateful to thousands of people who shared a part of their lives with a stranger. I don't know your name or much about you, but no blog or book exists without your contributions. Not only have you given your stories to me, but you've listened to mine.

Those who subscribe to my weekly blog have meant the world to me. Many of you write back and tell me how much you've enjoyed my writing. I can't thank you enough. This group also includes people who told me they'd missed my stories when I took breaks. Many writers suffer from the 'imposter syndrome.' Whenever I sent out a blog, I wondered why anyone would want to read such drivel. You lifted me more often than you know!

I'm grateful to Rob Holbert, the co-publisher of Lagniappe Daily newspaper, for publishing forty-eight of my blogs in his paper in 2024. I've appreciated his advice and support. His readers often stopped me on the street to tell me how much they enjoyed my column. Most of them didn't even know about the blog.

By the way, I don't think Rob would have even known about my blogs if my good friend, Ann Davis, hadn't harassed Rob when I was writing blogs with a political bent. Ann and Sam Davis have been a lifeline to Lane and me.

I started writing the Uber stories because of my friends in the Rotary Club of Mobile and their weekly meetings. Their encouragement to '*Tell us an Uber story*' prompted me to start the blog. After all, I also wanted to eat my lunch!

I'm grateful to Msgr. Bill Skoneki for writing the *Foreword* for this book. I've admired his written homilies and appreciated his support over the last thirty years.

When I first began writing the blogs, I shared them with a long-time friend I met years ago when we were active with the Alabama Jaycees. Jerry Taff helped edit many of my first efforts. He wrote a wonderful blurb supporting this book and me. Jerry often believed in me when I wasn't sure I would ever become something important. His friendship is worth more to me than he'll ever know.

While many of our friends have greatly supported this project, two of my lifelong buddies have meant the world to me. Both became Uber drivers and understood the challenges and rewards. First, Ben Hill has been a great friend for over fifty years. We've been through a lot together, and his support for this book has meant the world to me.

Second, Bud Malec, another high-school and lifelong friend, has been driving for Uber for almost as long as I have. I cannot tell you how many nights we spent talking to each other while waiting for rides. It is funny that many of our mutual passengers thought we were the same person. I guess our age and gray hair confused them. Bud and I shared many life conversations during those road hours.

I often tell my riders about life's challenges to Lane and me. But I always end the conversations with these facts. I've been married for more than forty-four years to Lane. She has put up with the craziness of our life and all its nuances. We have five wonderful children who are married to five great spouses. We recently welcomed our ninth healthy grandchild into this world. We have great friends and opportunities to make the most of our time on earth. We are blessed, and I wouldn't trade our lives with anyone else.

Finally, I owe all of my blessings to God. Even with our challenges, I can reach out to Him, ask for help and forgiveness, and give thanks for all He has done for me. I am truly blessed!

TABLE OF CONTENTS

FOREWORD

One of the things I still miss from my fourteen years in Auburn working with college students is Open St. Mike's Night, an annual talent show sponsored by the Auburn Catholic Campus Ministry. I participated in that show almost every year, either singing and/or participating in some skit or comedy routine. Performing was always fun and a great way to work with and get to know different students. Open St. Mike's Night had another personal benefit—it often exposed me to music I had never heard before. One year, a song by Ben Rector immediately caught my attention. Checking out his music, I discovered that Ben Rector was a storyteller singer like Harry Chapin, one of my beloved artists from the 1970s. The first Ben Rector song I heard, '*The Men That Drive Me Places*,' is still one of my favorites. In it, Rector tells the stories of two different men, Howard and Danny, who each transported him to one of his performances. After learning more about their struggles and their accomplishments, Rector sings this chorus, *"Why am I the only one who knows I'm half the man of the men who drive me places?"*

I met Tommy Fulton over 30 years ago when I served as a priest at St. Dominic Church in Mobile. He was not an Uber driver. I don't think I actually knew what he did for a living. What struck me most about Tommy back then was his large, active family, especially his children attending St. Dominic School. He and I had many conversations about his commitment to and involvement in Toastmasters. I left Mobile for Auburn in 2005, not returning until 2019 to become rector of the Cathedral in downtown Mobile. I was pleasantly surprised to learn that Tommy and his wife now lived in the next block behind the Cathedral. And I soon learned he had become a man who drove people places.

The baseball legend Yogi Berra once remarked, *"You can observe a lot by just watching."* Tommy has observed a lot by driving people around these past eight years. This book is a compilation of some of those observations—the victories and failures, wisdom and foolishness, and ups and downs of a broad spectrum of people riding in a car together. Having read Tommy's blog and newspaper column over the past few years, I recognize some of the stories and remember some of the lessons learned. Reading them a second time has led me to some different insights, not just about Tommy and his riders but also about my own perspectives on life.

The encounters shared in this book are conveniently divided into sections. Being a priest, the section labeled faith initially caught my eye. Other sections also captured my attention: humor, life balance, and conflict, to name a few. I recommend reading only a few entries at a time. Skipping around from section to section isn't a bad idea, either. Just as Tommy never knew who he might be picking up next, one cannot predict how reading about the lives of others might help us better live our own.

I have only been an Uber passenger twice in my life, once each year for the past two years. Nothing profound happened to me during either of those encounters. Tommy's experience with Uber has been much different than mine, thanks to thousands of interactions with others in his driving. Like Ben Rector's Howard, he has made a *'future out of hustling'* and listening and learning from others. He has many good stories to tell and much wisdom to share. Enjoy riding along with him.

Father Bill Skoneki

Rector, Cathedral-Basilica of the Immaculate Conception, Mobile

PROLOGUE

I have lived a full life, but not nearly all of it. My dad was an air traffic controller with the U. S. Air Force. My brother, sister, and I spent our early years in Cincinnati, Ohio, Okinawa, and Wichita, Kansas. After the death of my mother's father, Thomas W. Finch, we moved to Mobile, Alabama, to live out most of our lives.

My grandfather started his family business, Finch Warehousing and Transfer, Co., Inc., in 1933 on Mardi Gras Day in downtown Mobile during the Great Depression. I wrote another book about adventures in a family business, *'An Act of Congress - The Real-Life Story of Power and Politics In Family Business.'*

I began my post-college career in the family business. I was very active in several community and political organizations. I married a beautiful and intelligent woman, Lane Young, with whom we raised five very successful children. Those children have been blessed with wonderful spouses and have given us nine grandchildren.

God has been very good to us. That doesn't mean that life has been easy. Nobody's is. My sister, Terry, died in a car wreck in 1977. My parents taught us how to handle grief and heartache. But they also taught me how to persevere through tough times.

Our family business thrived—mostly. I became president at the age of twenty-nine. Again, I've covered the details in my previous book. After thirty years of lawsuits and tragic family discord, the business closed and left my wife and me with millions of dollars gone.

At the age of fifty-nine, Lane and I started over. We moved from our large home into a one-room loft in downtown Mobile. We thought we would try it for a year. We stayed there for eight. I began a career as the development director for the Little

Sisters of the Poor. Lane became the secretary for the Cathedral of the Immaculate Conception and was the wedding coordinator there.

"Why did you start driving for Uber?" many folks asked me.

So, here's the story.

My beloved, note-free Ford F-150 Crew Cab began its death spiral. It was time for a new vehicle. Unfortunately, that meant a car payment. I discussed our situation with Lane.

"Well," she said, "you can drive for Uber!"

My head began spinning. After all, I had been a successful businessman and a political and community leader. Had my life declined to that level?

"I'm not driving for Uber!" I told her. (I'm not sure I said that out loud, but my memory might be fuzzy.)

Two Sundays later, I purchased a used 2013 Hyundai Santa Fe and qualified to share rides with the public! I even bought two dozen barf bags that my research told me I needed. Further research told me that I should begin driving on a traditionally un-busy Sunday morning. Uber gave me no training to tell me what happened on the app when I got a request.

So, I sat in my car and stared at the app. Then, it happened! *Ding!* A box came up on my phone, which I immediately punched. Next, a map showed me where to pick up my rider. It was a dreary, rainy morning, which was perfect for me to learn with less traffic.

My first rider was staying at the Renaissance Riverview Hotel, less than a mile away. As I drove up under the covered valet area, I saw my rider, a young man with a backpack.

He hopped into the back seat and said, "Thanks for the ride! I'm not going far. I just didn't want to walk in the rain."

Two blocks later, I dropped him off at the Battle House. I thanked him for riding with me and explained that he was my first rider.

As I drove off, I looked at my app to see how much money I earned! To my dismay, it said, *'You have not driven far enough to earn a fee.'*

My first ride was free. I hoped this was not a sign of things to come. I would drive for Uber on nights and weekends while working full-time at the Little Sisters. Each week, I attended the Downtown Rotary Club membership luncheon.

Every luncheon started with my table-mates asking me to 'tell us an Uber story!' After several weeks, I started writing those stories as blogs on my website. Eventually, and surprisingly, I reached almost five hundred subscribers. One of those subscribers was the Co-Publisher of the Lagniappe News, the largest newspaper in Mobile, Alabama.

Rob Holbert was kind enough to publish my blog for a year, even after my wife and I had 'retired' to Gulf Breeze, Florida, to be near our two oldest daughters and their families.

I continue to write my weekly blog, which comes out every Tuesday. This book is a compilation of eighty columns over the last several years. People ask me how I get all these stories. At the time of this book release, I've had more than 19,000 passengers from at least 67 countries in my car. I'm amazed at the stories these wonderful folks have provided to me. And I'm grateful for the experience!

CHAPTER 1
ADVERSITY

IT'S ADDICTING!

You've met him before. I know you have. You don't necessarily know him by name, but he has been in your life at some point. Addiction is all around us. Whether it's a friend, a family member, or a casual acquaintance, the details differ, but the damage is all too common.

* * *

Wednesday at 9:00 pm. The Uber app told me to appear in front of a gay-oriented bar in downtown Mobile. A '40-something' year-old man hopped into the front seat.

"Just so you know, I'm not gay. My beautiful, twenty-nine-year-old girlfriend likes to go to gay bars because nobody messes with her there," he proclaimed. As if to prove his point, he pulled out a picture of her on his phone. She was a pretty woman.

"This is the end of our relationship! I'm through with her antics! It happens everywhere we go. One of her 'men' friends approached her and gave her a hug...not a quick hug...one of those extended hugs that says there is more to this relationship than just friendship.

"I made it clear to her that she leaves with me right now, or I'm taking an Uber home. I told her that if it came to that, this was the end of us!"

He lived in north Mobile County, so we had about forty-five minutes ahead. He told me that he was divorced, with three kids, and had run his own business in the past. That was, until he became addicted to opioids, went through rehab, and lost his business. His addiction and rehab lasted more than five years. His best friend was still addicted to opioids and often tried to get him to do drugs with him. He refused, which has

7

dimmed their relationship.

"I saw my life going downhill and couldn't stop until nothing was left. I don't want to live like that anymore. Tonight showed me the reality that I need to start all over again."

At that point, he showed me a series of texts he was currently receiving from his girlfriend. She was begging him to forgive her as she drove about twenty minutes behind us.

"She's so drunk... I can't believe she's driving. This is crazy!"

He told me she was still married to some European guy, even though she was living with him now. He seemed to be determined to break off this relationship. He wanted to bring back some sanity in his life and begin the effort to regain some sort of positive relationship with his kids.

He was quiet for the moment. He had been thinking about this move for a lot longer than tonight. She was merely an extension of his addiction. He was desperate to regain some level of normalcy in his life. I told him that he was in my prayers.

* * *

You would know someone in your life who is going through this chaos, too. Maybe it's you. Or perhaps it's family or friends. Please know that I'm praying for you, too.

"A WASTE OF LIFE"

The original *Rocky* movie is still the best one, in my humble opinion. It has a special place in my heart for reasons I'll share in a future edition. I'll use a line from that movie to tell this story for now.

I'm sure you've seen this part of the movie several times. Some of my riders exemplify this scenario. Rocky was a nobody, just taking up space at this local gym. Mick had removed Rocky's contents from a locker and placed them in a bag on 'skid row.' Rocky questions Mick as to why he's so abrasive to him.

Mick: *You had the talent to become a good fighter, but instead of that, you become a legbreaker to some cheap, second-rate loan shark!*

Rocky: *It's a living.*

Mick: *IT'S A WASTE OF LIFE!*

* * *

Shortly after starting my ride-share experience, Uber dinged me to go to a nightclub. It was very late on a Friday night. There were only three or four cars out front. I waited for my rider to come through the front door. I called him to see if he realized that I'd arrived.

"Just wait there... I'll be out in a minute!" he said.

A few minutes later, he responded the same way, so I made a third call.

"I'm coming out now!" he snarled. Then, he approached my car. "I've still got business in there. Cancel the ride!"

* * *

A few weeks later, I got another ding at the same bar. This time, it was about 12:30 pm on a Saturday. When I arrived, I saw it was the same guy. He told me to take him to another bar about 4-5 miles away.

At least he seemed pleasant this time. He had become my most prolific rider.

I didn't know much about the history behind his life, but I recognized waste when I saw it.

I picked him up at a dive in a rough part of town late one weeknight. He was visibly upset.

I asked him, "What's going on? Is everything okay?"

"No, everything's not okay! I'm divorced and lonely. I can't seem to build any relationship with a woman. It only takes a couple of dates before I realize I don't want her or she's not interested in me. I guess there isn't anyone out there for me." He was close to tears.

I didn't say it out loud, but I'm pretty sure his problem should have been obvious, especially to him. What woman wants to be with a man whose primary recreation is drinking? He told me later that he uses Uber because it's substantially cheaper than DUIs and wrecks, which has cost him tens of thousands of dollars over the years. He has a good job and seems productive, but his life changes daily at quitting time.

It was a few days before Thanksgiving weekend. I picked him up this time, and a young man accompanied him. He introduced me to his fourteen-year-old son. This was the first time I had driven him anywhere other than to or from a bar. I built some hope. Maybe there was something here to change his direction. They seemed to enjoy each other's company genuinely.

He asked me to stop at a gas station on the way home. "I need to pick up some chips from this place and get something for my son. His favorite wine is there. Just kidding!" (*He did get a bottle of wine.*)

While he was in the store, I talked with the son.

He said, "I can't wait until this weekend! Mom is letting me stay with Dad for two nights in a row. She never lets us do that! We're going to watch the *Iron Bowl* together! This will be our best time ever!"

I hoped so for both of them.

As luck would have it, Uber dinged me to pick up the Dad about a week later from a bar. "How was the Iron Bowl with your son? I bet y'all really celebrated the win!" I said.

"Well, my TV started giving me some trouble. I didn't want us to miss the game, so I dropped him off at one of his friends and went to a sports bar."

This news broke my heart. I kept seeing the enthusiasm on the face of that kid. I've picked his Dad up several times since then. He's been promoted at his job. I guess that's good, but I hope he'll see how much different his life could be someday. I hope his son grows up to have a 'full' life. I hope they have a great relationship. The odds are tougher, but both can avoid a 'waste of life.'

Throughout my life, I've met many people with life challenges. Some of them never defeat their demons. A lot of them do! The thing is, the successful folks never give up fighting. I keep all of them in my prayers, and I'm asking you to do the same. They need us.

HALFWAY HOME!

I've been driving for Uber since January of 2017. As of now, I've given more than 4,500 rides, probably more than 9,000 people. The rides I describe in this issue stand out to me because they all happened within a week or so of each other.

I picked up a young man recently from the Salvation Army. He needed a ride to one of the chemical plants for his job. He was recovering from an opioid addiction and was working hard to normalize his life. He was staying at the shelter and would take an Uber to work because it helped his wife. She needed their only car to transport their kids. He dripped with sincerity and wanted to keep his really good job. There were real people who cared about him. He felt it and didn't want to let them down.

A few weeks ago, I picked up another young man who had been through a period of addiction when he was in his early 20s. He would take Uber to his job. He lived in an old trailer that his boss owned. The guy was kind enough to help him when he was down, and even though the trailer was not in great shape, my rider was very grateful for a place to live. He'd been clean for six years now. He worked a lot, and even though the trailer was in bad shape, he went out of his way to ensure it was clean. Obviously, he was ambitious and took care of the little things that many folks would take for granted.

* * *

I got a ding to pick up yet another young man. He was in a halfway program and sold home products door-to-door. It was one of the few jobs he could get because of his criminal background. He used to sell meth on the street. He was also a user. When I picked him up, he had just completed a very successful sale of the home product.

I was curious, so I asked him, "Why did you get into drug sales in the very beginning, and what caused you to decide you needed/wanted to stop?"

He explained, "It was way too easy to make money. I could buy meth from a dealer for $185.00 and turn around and sell it for $2,500.00. It was in huge demand because it was effective in getting them high. I sold them some terrible stuff, but I only used the best myself; crystal meth."

"Then, what made you give up that life?"

"My girlfriend's mother turned me in. At first, the judge offered me this halfway program, but I wasn't interested in it at all." He continued, "A short time after that, I was going in for my drug test, and when they searched my wallet, they found a baggie with old, molded meth in it. I don't know why it was there, because I had been checked before and it wasn't found. My only guess is that God put it there somehow. The judge no longer gave me an option. He required me to go through the halfway house program. It has connected me with my faith, and I'm very grateful for the change in my life. That's why I think God put that meth in my wallet."

* * *

Years ago, I served on the Board for a home for drug and alcohol-addicted women. Each month, one of the women came to our luncheon and gave their testimony. After a while, I started to suspect that some were just mouthing the words. One of the caregivers told me that sometimes they would learn the right words to say without really understanding their meaning or the fundamental commitment that came with those words.

For the first two gentlemen I talked about above, I sincerely believed their words. They were real. I hope the third guy means his words. I pray that he meant them. If he didn't, he would not only fail himself, his family, and his friends but could cause significant damage to anyone he runs across.

In each of the first two situations, the guys had someone to mentor them, someone who believed in them. That seemed to be a key, at least to me. Sometimes, the key to individual success is knowing that someone cares. Several weeks ago, I met a girl on one of my rides—a sister who was supporting her brother, whom we picked up from jail. She is making a difference in his life.

Find someone who needs it—support—,and make sure they know you care.

"ESCAPE TO A NEW LIFE!"

I picked her up in Theodore, standing about four houses from the pickup address indicated on my Uber app. She waved the yellow light icon Uber put on the screen to help identify the rider. It was about 7:30 pm. Most riders choose the rear, passenger-side door. Uber suggests that the single rider sit there. "Kaitlin" chose the front seat.

"Do you mind if I sit here?" she asked after making herself comfortable. It was obviously a rhetorical question.

My response, "You can drive if you want to!" usually gets a laugh. This time, just a mild chuckle.

"Do you know where you're taking me?"

"I know it's about an hour away. Our app only tells me once I pick you up. I see we're going to Rabun, Alabama."

"I'm running away from my boyfriend. I'm starting my life over for about the fourth time. I'm not very good at relationships."

I guessed that Kaitlin was in her early 30s. She told me she was an athlete in college, but after an injury, she had to quit playing. I don't know what happened to her after that, but she moved in with someone who impressed her. Unfortunately, they grew apart, probably from a lack of commitment by either of them.

She found another guy who seemed a little more serious. Enough that they created a child together. That chased him away.

Finally, a new gentleman came into her life. They married, and she hoped she had finally found a keeper. Kaitlin admitted that both were still partiers, even with a child to raise. She knew it was time to grow up.

Even though Kaitlin enjoyed marijuana and drinking with him, it was not what she wanted for her child. So she quit, and after a period of sobriety, she gave her husband an ultimatum. "It's either the weed or me." He chose the weed.

I asked, "Is that the guy we just left?"

"No," she said. "The guy I just left is an alcoholic. When we first met, he was wonderful. So sweet to my kid and me." She was quiet for a few moments.

"He began to drink more and more. About three months ago, we fought, and he broke my nose. I should have left then. I didn't."

"Was he at home when we left?" I asked.

"He was passed out. He won't know I'm gone until tomorrow. Once he's out, he's out. I don't think it will matter to him."

She explained that she had taken her child to a friend and would pick up her car from the repair shop in Rabun. She had a place to stay temporarily with her child. She had a good job in Mobile but hoped to restart a relationship with her family.

"I'm committed to raising my daughter by myself. I don't pick partners very well."

We reached her destination. She thanked me for listening to her woes.

I told her that she would be in my prayers. I've said that to a lot of my riders. My Men of St. Joseph prayer group brothers will vouch for that.

"CHEAP AMBULANCE!"

I got a ding to pick up a gentleman at Mobile Infirmary Patient Discharge. We'll call him Richard. The aides helped him into the back seat of my car.

"I'd ask you how you're doing, but I'm sure it's better than when you entered," I said. "How are you feeling?"

"I feel pretty good. I've been in this time for three days. I've had fairly major problems with my heart in the past, so when I started feeling bad, the doctor insisted that I go to the hospital. I guess I'm okay," he replied.

After some small talk, I noticed he was going to the Saraland Shopping Center. I asked, "Do you need a ride home from there? I'll be happy to wait if you need."

"I live at the end of the sidewalk. It's covered, so it's a good place for me. I've been trying to get up with a few nearby churches, but no one's there when I stop by."

When we arrived, he pointed to a few clothing racks in front of the store at the end of the shopping center. "There's all my stuff, right where I left it." He pointed to a chair and three or four bags. He seemed perfectly happy to be there. After a few more minutes of small talk, I left him there.

* * *

A few days later, I got another request to pick up Richard at Mobile Infirmary. *Dang, I hope he is okay.* I waited for the aides to bring him back.

They asked, "Are you looking for Richard?"

This 'Richard' was a much bigger fella, not the same guy. They struggled to get him in the car.

We don't know the destination until we've indicated on the app that we've picked up our rider. This Richard was going to Saraland. What a coincidence. He was very personable.

"I've been in the hospital for two weeks. I can't wait to get home," Richard told me. He told me all his maladies. He'd had it rough.

"I've done a lot of traveling in my life. I've traveled all over this country in a truck."

I asked, "Are you retired?"

"No, I used to ride with a friend of mine. She's retired now. I've been on disability all my life. When I was 22 months old, I got hit in the neck with an axe head. A guy was chopping wood and didn't see me. The axe slid off the wood. I had to re-learn how to talk and walk, even at that young age." He continued to explain his life experiences to me. He was grateful to the people who had helped him all his life. He was especially complimentary of Bill Barber, who spent his life helping people with disabilities.

Mr. Barber told me once, "You're not special; you just need a little help. I'll help you make a living. And he did!"

We were getting closer to his trailer. When we passed the Saraland Shopping Center, I looked to my right. At the end of the sidewalk, I saw the previous 'Richard' sitting in a chair, relaxing next to a couple of racks of clothing on sale.

After we arrived at the trailer park, I helped him climb the cinder block steps in front of his trailer. Little kids played in the driveway and seemed genuinely happy to see Richard.

"Yep, they've kinda adopted me!"

* * *

Sometimes, we take people to the hospital. Once, I got dinged to pick up a young lady in downtown Mobile. When I pulled up, she motioned for me to lower the front passenger window.

"Can I sit up front and lower the seat all the way back?" she asked. "I've got severe sciatic pain, and I need to go to the emergency room at USA Hospital."

She was in obvious pain and winced every time I hit the slightest bump. Still, she carried on the conversation.

"I'll bet you've never had anyone in this position on your Uber rides. How long have you been doing this?"

"About six and one-half years. I've had more than 16,000 riders from at least 68 different countries. But, yeah, you're the first I've had in this position," I answered.

"Well," she said, "I live in Egypt as a missionary. I've also lived in Afghanistan and a few other countries."

We engaged in one of the two discussion topics that most polite conversations avoid—not politics.

"My parents are Catholic. Of course, neither has attended church more than a few times in the last twenty years. You know how Catholics are," she went on. "They're baptized as babies and think they just have to do works occasionally to reach heaven."

I could not resist it. "I'm Catholic, and I hear that argument constantly from non-Catholics. I can honestly say that I don't know a single Catholic who believes they can get to heaven on works alone!"

Believe it or not, the conversation continued on a civil note as we rolled up to the emergency entrance at USA. I told her that my Catholic Men's group meets the following day. "The Men of St. Joseph will pray for your complete recovery at our meeting tomorrow."

"My name is Linda. I appreciate your prayers very much. I'll keep you and your group in mine. Thank you!"

I decided to talk a little about politics the next time I would see her. Or maybe I would not.

"ATTITUDE OF GRATITUDE!"

We have so many reasons to be grateful! In one of the upcoming chapters, "Caught Short," I mentioned how many times people have stepped up to help me during my life. I am grateful for that. But I'm constantly amazed by the attitude I've witnessed from many rideshare passengers.

This time, I picked up a gentleman from a truck stop in South Mobile County. This truck stop featured a Wendy's restaurant. At first, I couldn't find my rider, and his phone wasn't accepting messages. One of the workers walking through the parking lot thought the gentleman might be the guy who slept in the dumpster area last night. At that moment, my rider walked toward me with his duffle bag.

"That's him," said the employee. "The one with the crutches."

He struggled to get in the back seat. "It's been a long night," he said. "I drive trucks, even though I only have one leg. Thankfully, it's my right leg, so I can work with all the pedals!"

He went on, "I disagreed with my boss on 'company policy,' so he cut me loose down here. I'm from Oklahoma, and my brother got a bus ticket for me to get home. I couldn't find him yesterday, so I slept behind the dumpster last night. I already have another truck driving job set up when I get back. Sometimes, life has been tough, but I always bounce back with God's help!"

I could tell he was a nice person by his good attitude.

* * *

I picked up a family at a used car dealership a few months later. The mother got in the front seat, and everyone else piled into the back. One of the kids was sniffling. None of them looked happy.

"All of you pray!" she said. "We'll get through this."

She looked at me. "We were supposed to get a car today, but something came up on the credit report at the last minute. It just wasn't meant to happen today..." she trailed off.

Then, she spoke again, "But God is with us and will take care of our needs. He always has. We'll get a car when we're supposed to. That's what we pray for."

Again, this was a great attitude of gratitude!

* * *

The next week, I picked up a young man working on the waterfront. I always ask, "So, how's your day going?" and I did so this time, too.

"It's getting better all the time," he said. "I've just started a new job at the shipyard. I worked in temp labor until last week. I spent a few months in jail for DUI. They're pretty serious about that in Florida."

He continued, "I've been sober for 11 months now. It didn't seem like it then, but the DUI was probably the best thing that's happened to me. I've changed my whole life. Now, with this job, I should be able to get my own place to live and get my own car!"

I couldn't tell what he was like before the DUI, but I liked what I saw of this man now. I dropped him off at the Waterfront Rescue Mission.

"You're on your way! I'm so happy for you! Keep it up!" I told him. Which of us was more upbeat? I was not sure.

Good attitude.

* * *

Later that day, I picked up another guy with an attitude. He was getting off at his new job.

"How was your day?" I asked.

"Long day, but I love my job!" he said. "It wasn't easy for me to get a job because I was in federal prison for several years.

21

I was in for financial crimes, wire fraud, things like that." He quieted down, settling into a comfortable silence.

He spoke again, "I have a special knack for machine maintenance and have served at several prisons using those skills. That eventually paid off when I got out. Believe it or not, another Uber driver is responsible for me getting this job. I helped her with her car and went with her to the dealership. When we pulled up, I asked them if they needed anyone. I got the job!" he exclaimed, sounding proud of himself. "Now, all I need is to find a place to live. No apartment complex will accept a convicted felon, especially over here in Baldwin County."

After a slight pause, he continued, "Right now, I'm sleeping on my mother's living room floor. That's not fair to her. Also, my brother lives there, and I'd like to find a place nearby for him and me. Mom deserves a place to herself. I want to be near enough to be there when she needs me."

He said he could find a place in Mobile, but that was out of the question. "One of the things I've learned is that I need to change three things to stay out of trouble. My location, my 'friends,' and my attitude. I'm doing that."

He paused again, then said, "I was raised Catholic but went to several different religions over the years. I know I need to get back into a church, but I'm not sure where to go."

We talked for a little longer about possible options. I knew God would forgive me, and I hoped my former pastor would, too. I gave him my Little Sisters of the Poor business card with the name of a nearby Catholic church and the pastor's name. I didn't know if he would go, but I hoped so.

I told him, "I'll keep you in my prayers."

He answered, "Thanks. I know that God is always there for me no matter what else happens. That's the one thing I've always been grateful for."

That's a pretty good attitude right there!

"IT'S IN THE BLOOD!"

They're saving lives—lots of them. It's not unusual to pick up folks about to give their plasma or take them home after donating—their reasons for contributing range from supplementing their income to helping their fellow citizens in need.

In this chapter, I'll comment on three of them.

South Alabama had a football game on Tuesday night some time ago. I had just dropped off a fan who parked his car off campus to avoid the traffic. After maneuvering through the game traffic, I got a ding to pick up someone at one of the USA dorms. Now, I had to get back on campus.

"Sorry it took me so long to get to you," I said. "This football traffic is brutal!"

"Why do we have football traffic?" he said.

I figured that he was not a football fan.

"I've got something to take care of tonight," he told me.

I took several alternate routes to get us off campus and on our way. I drove toward the plasma donation center.

"It's part of my student budget, unfortunately. I run by here when I'm running low on funds. It's enough to help me finish out the month." He told me there were a lot of students that went there.

So, even if they're only looking out for themselves to save themselves from financial strife, they're unknowingly saving the lives of so many others.

There are also times when I overhear (eavesdrop on) people's phone conversations. This next guy is an example.

I picked him up at another plasma donation facility. He was already in conversation on his phone.

"I'm doing the best I can right now! I can't work for some of these jerks," he told his significant other on the phone.

I heard her respond, "You've had three jobs in the last six months! You can't work with any of them!" Then she hung up on him.

He immediately got another call. It was his father.

"I can't get my car fixed yet, so I'm wasting money driving around in an Uber," he said. (Thanks, my friend, you ain't no day at a park yourself!)

He continued, "She won't let me come back home until I get a job and get my car back. At this rate, it'll take six months!"

He had got an extra stop on this ride. We arrived at Circle K. My rider got snacks and a six-pack of Miller Lite. He might need to add a month or two to his timeline.

But it was this third guy that got to me. This ride took place a few weeks later. I picked him up at the same plasma facility I mentioned above. He seemed a little down.

"How's your day going?" I asked.

"This is one of the worst weeks of my life," he said.

"I'm sorry to hear that," I answered. "What's going on?"

"My nephew was killed a couple of days ago. Someone shot him five times and left him in the 'valley' to die." (I guessed the 'valley' referred to a part of town.)

He continued, "I lost my big brother earlier this year in a car accident. My dad died just before that. To make matters worse, I was working at a national chain restaurant that went out of business at my location. It was a good job. They said I could transfer to the other site, but the doors were closed when I showed up there. They went under, also."

He spoke again, "I started another job this week and had only been to work a couple of times when my nephew died. Now, I don't have enough money to pay my rent."

"What's happening with your new job?" I asked.

"They've been great. They understand what I'm going through, and they're holding the job for me. That's why I have to do the 'plasma thing' to survive."

He told me he believed in God and believed in prayer, but he still thought he wouldn't feel normal for a long time. Unlike the previous gentleman, this guy was trying. He just kept getting knocked down. I offered prayers from my men's group, the Men of St. Joseph.

* * *

When I think about these three rides, I think about each rider's situation and what they're going through. I think about how messy life can be. I don't think anyone escapes the challenges and the heartbreaks.

Later came Thanksgiving. Thanksgiving is my favorite holiday. We might wonder why and how some people do not feel grateful right now. That's not me, though. I don't have to look far to count the blessings.

So, what blessings come from my three riders? Well, for one, there are cancer patients and other recipients who will live because these gentlemen gave their life-giving blood. And, while these guys will likely never meet their recipients, somebody is thanking God for them.

"HOPE!"

It was December 2023. Friday nights were different from the rest of the week. At least, that's the way I've seen it as an Uber driver. This particular Friday, which I discuss below, was no exception.

I pulled up to a house just north of Mobile city limits. At least in the Griswold tradition, Christmas had undoubtedly come to this house. I had trouble seeing my passenger until he appeared through thousands of multi-colored lights.

"Are we going to pick up some more Christmas lights?" I asked.

He laughed. "No, I think we've got enough. My mom takes this very seriously."

"I get it," I said. "There is another enthusiast right down the street!"

"Yep, that's my aunt. They're friendly competitors!" he told me.

He had an extra stop to pick up seafood beside a liquor store. As I pulled into the parking lot, the only open spot was in front of the liquor store. I turned off my lights so I wouldn't blind the two men standing two feet in front of my hood. A third man approached one of them, who pulled a baggie from his jacket and filled the new man's 'papers' with the contents.

As he lit up, a group of young people walked by the trio. A couple of them were at most ten years old. It's just part of the 'community,' which seems sad. I hoped they had better examples in their lives.

* * *

Uber sent me to pick up a young lady in Midtown Mobile. We passed a homeless person with a cardboard sign, a frequent sight. We were both aware of his history. He'd been arrested at least two dozen times for various offenses.

He had tremendous artistic talent but seemed incapable of benefitting from it. Countless people tried to help, but he was unwilling or unable to accept the help.

"I know another man who is often homeless by his own choice. He received a huge lawsuit judgment from a workplace accident a few years ago," she explained.

"He spent all of that on drugs and women. Now, he spends his time on the streets. We've all tried to help him, but he refuses to change. He says he has no hope for his future and sees no reason to try."

* * *

Later, Uber sent me to a 'big box' store in West Mobile.

"Thanks for waiting," the guy said. "A lot of drivers don't like driving to the middle of nowhere, so I sometimes have difficulty getting a ride."

We were heading toward the outskirts of Chunchula, Alabama.

"My truck is broken down. I'm gonna fix it myself as soon as I get enough money to buy the parts. I work at the store we just left. I use the truck to transport cars all over the place. I also have a landscaping business that I use the truck for," he declared.

"You're quite the entrepreneur!" I told him. "How old are you?"

"I'm nineteen. I have to stay busy. I've been through a lot of tough things in my life, and I'm trying to work my way out of them," he admitted honestly.

"Do you mind telling me about them?" I asked.

"I used to hang around some bad guys. I got shot a couple of years ago because I was in the wrong place at the wrong time. They weren't shooting right at me, but I got hit in my leg and my back from ricochets."

He went on, "Another time, I spent six days in jail. I got out with a two-year probation because I was a juvenile offender. I'm around guys who are still planning ways to get money illegally. I think they're stupid. I've seen what happens to these guys when they get caught."

I asked, "Do you mind telling me what got you into jail?"

He said, "I was with a couple of other guys in an armed robbery. I shouldn't have been with them, but I was."

"What about your parents? How did they react?"

"My mom died in 2019. My dad lives in another state. If it wasn't for my grandmother, I'm not sure what would have happened to me and my sister. She never gave up on me."

"So, what are your plans for the future?" I asked. "You don't appear to be afraid of hard work."

"First, I want to fix my truck. Then, I'd like to make enough money to go back to school. I'd really like to learn to work in radiology someday. I appreciated what those guys did when I had part of my intestine removed because of the bullet. At least, that's my hope!"

I dropped him off, as he said, in the middle of nowhere. I told him my men's prayer group would be praying for him. I knew he'd meet hundreds of obstacles ahead. I just hoped he beat them all.

As I drove off, I thought about the final lines in the movie *Shawshank Redemption*.

"I find I'm so excited I can barely sit still or hold a thought in my head.

I think it's the excitement only a free man can feel, a free man at the start of a long journey whose conclusion is uncertain.

I hope I can make it across the border.

I hope to see my friend and shake his hand.

I hope the Pacific is as blue as it has been in my dreams.

I hope."

"PINBALL WIZARD!"

I guess I was aging myself. I loved the old-fashioned pinball machines. You pull back the plunger, which let a silver ball load into the mechanism. Then, you use your experience to judge just the right amount of spring needed to get the ball started at the top of the sloped, glass-covered obstacle course.

Now, you place your thumbs on the top of the machine and your index fingers on the buttons on each side of the game. These digits control the flippers, a vital component of the challenge. Timing becomes your tool. Bumpers, bells, blinking bulbs, and bank shots control the action until that magic ball comes near your flipper.

For one split-second, you control the direction of the ball. With the proper 'bump,' you can determine the following route for the little silver sphere. Rookies and veterans ultimately suffer the same fate. The ball finds its way to the bottom of the maze and disappears down the same abyss. Gone and game over.

I'm sure most Uber drivers identify the same feeling from the rides we deliver. And no, I'm not talking about maneuvering through traffic on Airport Blvd., although that could be an adventure all its own. I'm talking about the people. Our dear riders!

Whether we are traveling a short distance or several miles to pick up our passengers, the rides themselves can differ significantly.

When I began driving Uber, I had a three-seat Hyundai Santa Fe, which made me eligible to carry a maximum of six passengers.

Once, I got a call to pick up at least that many from the Springhill area of Mobile. We headed to a wedding in North Mobile County. All but one passenger seemed appropriately dressed for the event. That young man wore shorts and a ratty

T-shirt.

"We need to make an extra stop on the way," he told me. "My sister is bringing my suit."

I figured out we might make it on time if everything went perfectly. The handoff took place in a gas station parking lot. His sister threw the more formal attire through the back window.

We reached our destination shortly after the outdoor wedding ceremony had begun. A policewoman stopped us about fifty yards away. Those properly-clad young folks hurried toward the back of the wedding attendees. However, our young man quickly disrobed halfway between the featured wedding couple and my car.

The officer and I watched in amusement as the late lad stood only in his socks and underwear, hopping on one foot, trying to jump into his formal slacks with both legs. He succeeded on his second attempt and bounced off the nearby cars and a tree or two before making his way to the sacred ceremony.

This is just one of the stories. People are different, so each time we 'pull the plunger,' our riders give us a unique experience.

* * *

A few weeks later, I picked up a young man on the way to a liquor store. He said, "I totaled my car recently, so I have to take Uber now."

"So, what happened," I asked.

"I hit the rear of a dump truck going 80 miles per hour."

"I'm assuming the dump truck was going substantially slower than that," I said.

"Yep. My fault all the way," he answered. "Now, it's even worse. My girlfriend is in the hospital. She hydroplaned off the interstate ramp a few days ago and landed in a culvert. She broke a lot of bones and is in the hospital learning how to walk again. We're lucky she's still alive."

"Wow, that's a lot to happen in such a short time!" I said.

"Not only that," he continued. "My ex-girlfriend wrecked her car about two weeks ago!"

* * *

I added him and everyone associated with him to my prayer list. I think they'd banged off of every bumper on his pinball table.

My next ride had to be better.

I pick her up on campus. As usual, I asked her how her day was going.

"It's OK, under the circumstances," she said.

Here we go. "So, what's going on? You don't sound like it's really OK."

She sighed. "My boyfriend and I were living together. We ran out of money and couldn't afford our shared apartment, so he moved back in with his parents. He lives in another state."

"Sounds tough. I'm sorry you're going through all that." I decided to relay the misfortunes of my previous rider with the mistaken idea that she would be grateful her woes were less.

"Well," she said, "I didn't mention that the dealership repossessed my boyfriend's car. Also, I had to move in with my dad."

"How's that going?"

"When I got to his house, he wasn't there. He was in jail for DUI, and the police impounded his car. He has no license now, so we don't have a car."

Maybe that's why you don't see those pinball machines around anymore. Her little silver sphere had been knocked around way too much. I couldn't let it end without one more try, though.

"So, how's your education going?" I asked her.

"Thank goodness, I'm making good grades. Just a couple more years, and I'll get control of my life. I don't need any more challenges!"

Maybe my rider would get some extra plays in her game when she learns how to punch those flippers. God knows she was getting enough lessons for now!

ON THE ROAD AGAIN!

I have a confession to make. It was 2024, and it had been some time since I hit the road to offer rides to people, as I had not driven for Uber since April of that year. Between then and now, I spent time commuting from my job in Mobile to my new residence in Gulf Breeze, Florida. My drive was about three hours a day, which didn't leave me any time or desire to ride-share.

I missed it.

So, I started again. It had been a week now, and I could remember what intrigued me so much about those rides. As always, it was the people! I had eleven rides that week. These are some of the stories from my passengers.

* * *

One rider was an active policeman from the West Side of Chicago. He traveled every few weeks as he approached retirement. In a couple of months, he was going to require arm surgery, which would require him to use his remaining time for rehabilitation.

His wife has already relocated to this area. She was a former Chicago police officer herself. She now taught in one of the local high schools. My rider told me she worked at a facility known for disciplinary challenges. He proudly remarked, "She has no problem handling any disruptions. Spend one day in the West Side of Chicago, and you will understand real disruptions!"

Together, they'd been refurbishing their home and looked forward to spending time on the boat he had rehabbed.

* * *

After dropping him off, I picked up another gentleman who needed assistance to get in my car. He was legally blind and had recovered from a stroke and previous heart surgery. His former girlfriend had helped him set up an appointment and a ride to an eye doctor.

"I assumed it would be too complicated and time-consuming to arrange, so I put it off way too long," he said. "My 'ex' lives in Denver, but she still cares enough about me to help. We get along better with the time and distance between us!"

* * *

My next ride was with a Miami businessman named Albert. He was the heir apparent in his family business. I love talking to people who are in family businesses, as I've had a ton of experience making big mistakes in that arena. Therefore, we had a great discussion, but as we talked, I could tell he believed his business would have no problems as it transitioned to the next generation.

He also mentioned how he worked with his two brothers-in-law. They did not have any formal written plan for the next generation, so I gave him a copy of my book, *An Act of Congress: The Real-Life Story of Power and Politics in Family Business.* He could read my book or write his own once he realized the consequences of unwritten plans and expectations.

* * *

Soon after I dropped off Albert, I got a ding to pick up Albert. As soon as I saw him, I knew it wasn't the same guy. Back-to-back Alberts was unusual.

My new rider had long dreadlocks and gold teeth. In other words, he was dressed very casually.

"A lot of people mistake my appearance as a thug. I understand why," Albert explained. "Here's a perfect example. I was mowing the grass at a local church a couple of weeks ago. A passing motorist stopped and asked if I wanted something to eat or drink. He said I was working so hard. I told him I was fine, but he still offered me money. I took it and gave it to a homeless person.

"He didn't realize that I was mowing the grass as a charitable act for the church. He learned his mistake when we met at a financial management training session a week later. Everything isn't always what it seems."

Indeed!

* * *

Later, Uber summoned me to downtown Pensacola to pick up a young man. He was a very friendly guy. I think he said he was from New York State.

"What are you doing down here?" I asked.

"I play hockey for the Pensacola Ice Flyers. I love it here. Our team stays in apartments right across the street from the Gulf. It's one of the most beautiful places I've ever lived!" He looked at me, then said, "However, I just got traded to the Macon Mayhem in Georgia yesterday. Macon is playing Pensacola here tomorrow. I've got to be careful not to pass the puck to my former teammates accidentally."

"I called my dad," he continued. "I told him they traded me for $1." His father advised him to play as long as he could, telling him, "Once you age out, you can never go back!"

* * *

The next day, I picked up a couple from one of the neighboring towns. The man hoped to move to a quiet, small Baldwin County, Alabama town.

He said, "I've stayed there several times, and it's one of the few places where people don't treat me like a freak. After I served my time in prison, that's something I've not had much luck locating."

As he spoke, I took in his appearance, noticing how he had massive facial tattoos, some resembling a skull. I hoped he and his girlfriend would find peace somewhere.

* * *

Finally, I picked up an older lady who looked like she was suffering and in pain as she approached my car. After I helped her into my car, she told me to wait for a man who would ride with us. I assumed the gentleman who sat next to her was her son.

She was moaning and softly crying. She was obviously in a lot of pain.

Her son explained, "The doctors repeatedly misdiagnosed her with anemia or anorexia. Eventually, someone realized she had cancer. Because it took them so long to diagnose her properly, the cancer has spread to her uterus, her bones, and several other organs. We're on the way to radiation treatments."

A song was playing on the radio from the 70s, and as she listened, she began singing it. She said that the music from that time made her happy. She was going to receive chemotherapy if the radiation didn't work. I offered to pray for them.

Then, I was back to driving. I won't say I didn't need the money. I will say that I needed the people, and I was fascinated by their stories. So, I guess, will you...

FOUR–PEAT!

Occasionally, Uber would provide a message to go with their request for service. The message warned us that the people paying for the ride could monitor our every move. This usually meant that a charity, a doctor's office, or a hospital was footing the bill.

One Saturday, I got four of those in a row. I must have been on a list. Technically, I received five of those. My first rider's name was 'general.' I picked him up twice that day. Since his name wasn't capitalized, I wasn't sure if it was a 'generic' passenger or a show of modesty.

I immediately liked 'general.'

"Is general your real name?" I asked.

"Yeah," he said. "My parents gave that to me."

I loved his attitude. He was the type that made you smile, a positive-attitude fellow. He was seventy. Our ages were similar (I was 69 then), and our outlook on life was a common factor. After a few minutes into our conversation, I realized our circumstances were drastically different.

You would never guess it from his demeanor, but 'general' had all kinds of health problems and was doing everything he could to defeat other life challenges. He did not let it get him down.

* * *

My next rider was a mother with a young boy. Within five seconds, I realized I would not want to be her opponent in a battle.

"I've had all I'm gonna take from those apartment people. Nobody should have to live in a building with as many problems as we've got! I got electrical problems so bad; I burnt up my new dryer just because of bad wiring."

During the short breaks in her 'presentation,' I tried to show my support.

"I hope everything works out for you soon," I said.

"Well, it's gonna work out, or they will be sorry. They ain't never messed with anybody like me. They said it would take at least a week to come in and replace the wiring. All I know is they need to get me another place to live during that time."

Sometimes, when countered with situations such as this, you just stare at the Uber map and watch the distance and time of arrival approach.

Time passed until I had to say my goodbyes, and I wished her the best. Her demeanor totally changed as she left the car.

"Thanks for the ride," she said. "Have a nice day!"

* * *

Next was a trip to a rehab center. The gentleman came flying down a sloped sidewalk toward my car.

"Are we bringing the wheelchair with us?" I asked.

"Nah, they'll get it later. Leave it there!"

'Richard' slowly made his way into my back seat.

"So, what's your name?" he asked.

Richard was one of those people who loved to say your name in almost every sentence. He told me he had fought through multiple battles over the past week—with his health insurance, the government, and the bureaucracy. The insurance company turned him down for the medications he'd been receiving for several months.

"Would you mind doing me a favor on our way?" he asked. "I need a pack of cigarettes."

It was on the way, so I stopped while he struggled to go inside.

"Tommy, I really appreciate your help! I'm gonna give you five stars and maybe a tip, if I can! By the way, this restaurant you're taking me to is fantastic. If you ever get a chance to eat there, Tommy, you should!"

We arrived a few minutes later at an all-you-can-eat Asian-American establishment. He struggled to exit my car.

"Tommy, I'm trying to decide whether to sit out front and have a cigarette before I go in or after. What do you think?"

My answer? "I hope everything works out well with your insurance. Have a great day!"

Ding! There he was again—'general' needed another ride.

"Turns out the place you took me didn't have what I needed. But I get another chance to ride with you!" he exclaimed.

You gotta love this guy.

I had nothing to complain about, though. One more ride for the day for me! Again, Uber warned me that the organization providing the ride may monitor my performance. The rider may also need assistance.

I saw him outside the grocery store waiting with one of those electric shopping carts. He had some obvious physical challenges. He was a veteran. He looked tired and described some of the tough times he had faced during the last several years.

We reached his apartment, and I grabbed all of his groceries. I waited for him at the door.

"Would you like me to bring your bags inside?" I asked.

He finally made it to the door. "Go ahead and put the bags inside. The door's unlocked," he spoke. "Just put them on the left."

I was shocked when I opened the door. There was no furniture. He had only a few full trash bags and a few random objects in the room.

"Last time I went to the hospital, someone broke in and took all my furniture."

I had a hard time sleeping that night. To be beginning a new year in a country that's supposed to be the most advanced ever? It troubled me.

He hadn't given up. Not yet. He had a few friends, but they had some challenges to face, too.

* * *

I rejoined two groups that week that were dedicated to helping those in need. One group offers prayers; the other offers action. We need both.

CHAPTER 2
CONFLICT

GET AWAY CAR—IT'S GOD'S PLAN!

What is the strangest ride you've given as an Uber driver? That's the #1 question my rideshare passengers ask me. This story is at least in the top three so far.

The app showed my rider was next to a Walgreens in Spanish Fort, about 3 minutes from me. As I arrived, I saw 'Kathy,' a thirty-ish young lady in jeans, standing behind the store. She had two or three laundry baskets and at least a dozen Walmart bags. Once we got everything loaded into the car, she explained that she needed to get to Pensacola right away.

She said she was in this predicament because her 'new' boyfriend had just broken up with her. This happened after she told him she was going back to her 'old' boyfriend. She had explained this to the guy just moments before, then asked him to take her to Pensacola so she could be with the other guy—the ex. Walgreens was as far as he would travel with her.

She said, "My old boyfriend had just been released from jail in New Orleans for the sixth time. 'Fahad' is from Pakistan. His family owns several service stations/convenience stores in the New Orleans area. Fahad's future ex-wife has a good relationship with the law enforcement folks in that area, which is how he keeps ending up in jail. She constantly has him arrested for various offenses (false charges!!!)." Karen was meeting Fahad in Pensacola to begin an extended vacation in Florida.

Fahad was a multi-millionaire who owned a Mercedes Benz G-car. He had recently crashed the car into an Audi, and it had just been repaired. She went on further to say that Fahad was good friends with the president of Pakistan, and every time he visited there, the Pakistani president met him at the airport. He spent three months each year in that country.

As we headed to Pensacola, she exclaimed that this was "God's Plan" and that "God never sleeps." Between her declarations that God wanted them to be together, she exhibited one of the most foul-mouths I've ever had in my car, and that's saying something.

In one of her stories, she suspected that Fahad's attorney was secretly working for his soon-to-be ex-wife and was monitoring them through his cell phone. She got so upset that she threw his iPhone out of the car window on the interstate. He said it was the reason for dumping her.

Fahad's attorney, shortly after, gave him a ride that suddenly ended at a police station, where Karen's suspicions were realized. The police arrested him again. (Fahad's nephew, waiting at the Pensacola hotel for us with the G-car, called Karen as we drove there. During their discussion, he told her that she shouldn't have thrown Fahad's phone out of the window, even with all that had happened. This added some level of legitimacy to her story, I guess).

Fahad's father had passed the businesses down to him. This included many commercial properties leased to other entities, such as fast-food stores. Somehow, Fahad's wife received at least five or six of these and was running them into the ground. Several had already gone under. She was supposedly doing this on purpose, just to hurt him.

As we approached the hotel, Karen again assured me that this was "God's Plan," which she explained she could determine because of her upbringing in Mississippi. (I'm not sure I got that, but it was her story). We arrived and transferred the laundry baskets and Walmart bags into the G-Car with the help of Fahad's nephew.

* * *

Even after thousands of rides, this one remained one of my most memorable.

Keep reading.

There are many more stories to come! It's 'God's Plan!'

TARGETED!

Sometimes, you can see emotion on the face and in the posture of your rider.

That night, as I pulled up in front of a shopping center, I wrongly assumed the gentleman was agitated at me, but I couldn't figure out why. He chose the front seat, and I could tell he was unhappy.

"How's your day going?" I asked.

"One of the worst days of my life I've had it! I'm leaving this country as soon as I can arrange a flight out," he answered.

"What's wrong?"

He explained, "My wife is crazy, and I've had all I can stand of her lunacy! We own a store in the mall, but the closest restroom is in Target, so I had just taken a quick break. When I returned just a few minutes later, my wife accused me of having 'carnal knowledge' with a woman in the bathroom while I was gone. I was only gone a couple of minutes. The woman, a mutual acquaintance, just happened to be walking by our store at that minute."

I asked, "Do you have a relationship with this woman?"

"No!" he said. "I only vaguely know her, but my wife always comes up with crazy ideas. I'm her third husband. We have a one-year-old child and another on the way. Even if I had wanted to do something with this woman, I was only gone for a few minutes. This is crazy!"

He then excused himself and got on the phone with a travel agent. He told the person he wanted to leave immediately and would be gone for at least thirty days. One of the destinations he mentioned to the agent was Casablanca. He spoke in some Arabic dialogue for most of the conversation, so I didn't know most of what he was saying.

When he finished the call, he continued our conversation. "We haven't been married very long, but we spend most of our time arguing. I'm getting a one-way ticket, and I'll have to decide what happens then."

"Does she know your plans?" I asked.

There was a pause, and I couldn't tell whether she knew he would be gone. He said he was Muslim, but I wasn't sure if his wife was of the same faith. I kept thinking that no matter the challenges, two children were involved. There had to be some way to slow this whole thing down.

"I'm going to pack up some important things, not very much, but things I know I will need. I'm not sure how quickly I can get a flight, but I'm leaving the house tonight and getting a hotel."

"Why don't you get the room and see how you feel in a few days? I don't pretend to know the situation, but things could look different after a few days. I know your children will need you. You may always regret being away when your new baby is born. You can still make the big decision later."

The remainder of the ride was quiet. I hoped that was a good sign, but he may have just wanted me to shut up. We reached our destination, but he sat in the car for a few minutes.

"I'll keep you and your family in my prayers," I promised.

He stared at me for a minute, then quietly said, "I appreciate that very much..."

HARVEY & BEERFEST

Since I began driving for Uber, one of the most frequently asked questions has been, "Do you ever feel unsafe?" I explain that I rarely feel unsafe myself.

One of the more intriguing follow-up questions comes from women. "Would you suggest that a woman become a driver?"

I usually answer, "If they can control where and when they drive, then I suppose it could work. But, if you ask whether I would suggest my wife or daughters do this, I would have to say 'No' in almost all cases."

While these following stories are somewhat 'atypical,' they still occur. This night was 'Beerfest' in downtown Mobile, and it remains one of my most lucrative days ever.

Hurricane Harvey had just hit Houston the day before. At 7:24 pm, I got a ding on my Uber app to pick up a young man who needed to drop by a couple of stores to buy some items for his kids arriving from Houston. They would stay for a few days in Mobile until their situation in Houston settled down.

I asked him, "Oh, how many kids do you have?"

He said, "Well, these are three of them, but I have eight total." He then started telling me about everything women could do to you. "You have to be really careful with them. They can really cause problems for men!"

He got a call from his former wife or girlfriend (not sure which), who told him she would be at his mother's house, where the kids were staying. She further told him she was bringing her boyfriend. His voice began to rise, as did his temper. (He told me after the call that he and this other guy had fought several months ago. My rider had received a black eye in the confrontation and was worried that he would have to defend his honor on his home turf.)

His anger continued to escalate as he kept questioning the woman about why she insisted on creating another lousy situation in front of their kids.

He told me he hadn't seen these kids in a year, and after we left Walmart, he was concerned that his purchases would not be enough. He asked that we stop at the dollar store before I dropped him off at his mother's house. Then, he returned to the car and said everything was too expensive. I tried to get him to concentrate on making his reunion with his kids the primary purpose of this visit and forget about all the distractions.

After I dropped him off, I kept thinking I might read about him in the news the next day.

* * *

Later that night, at about 12:45 am, I picked up a guy in downtown Mobile who had taken utmost advantage of the Annual Beer Fest. He told me he had to use Uber because he got a DUI a week ago. He was so drunk now that he could barely walk. I'm pretty sure he hadn't fully taken in the lessons from the DUI.

I would keep some emesis bags (throw-up) in my car, just in case. I informed my rider that if he needed one, he should take one. If he needed one but didn't use it, it could cost him $150.00 for the clean-up, and I don't want $150.00 that bad. He assured me he would not need it. He asked me to take him to Burger King first, then told me his mother had breast cancer. I felt terrible for him but was happy to get him home safely.

He told me he would check the app when sober and promised a nice tip. However, I'm not sure that ever actually happened.

To top off a record-breaking night, I got a ding at about 1:30 am to pick up a guy near Virginia Street and I-10. Unfortunately, there were no homes or businesses where he was, so I couldn't figure out what he was doing there.

He had been at Beerfest with two women and had argued with them. He thought the best thing to do would be to leave them and walk home since he had obviously had way too much to drink.

The problem was that he lived in Daphne, across the bay from downtown Mobile. He was heading in the opposite direction and had to pass the county jail and an incredible number of bail bonding places to end up where I picked him up. He said that was when he realized he was not in a good part of town.

As I explained, he would have had to walk through the tunnel, then across the causeway in the opposite direction, to accomplish that feat. He was very grateful that I picked him up.

He told me that he had been in the navy and was working toward being an air traffic controller. As we talked, he asked for life advice and seemed to listen very intently to me. I felt sorry for his immediate situation, but he was very polite and appreciative.

I hoped he would be more responsible now when directing aircraft throughout our skies.

I've had the chance to meet some women who have been driving for Uber and/or Lyft. They seemed to enjoy ride-sharing and keep themselves in safe situations as best they could. Truth be told, most of the guys did their best to avoid 'iffy' circumstances. 99% of my rides were great people, sometimes in not-so-great situations.

Every once in a while, though...sheesh!

COUPLES IN CONFLICT!

This weekend, I picked up a young lady at a downtown bar. Her boyfriend was standing beside her. He opened the door for her. She was crying. He said, "I'll be home in a little while. Why are you crying?"

She didn't answer.

He said, "I love you. I'll see you later."

"Are you ok?" I asked.

"My boyfriend is such a jerk!" she sobbed. "I'm a single mom of two kids. Everything is always my fault!" I could tell she didn't believe that last part.

We carried on with small talk. As I dropped her off, I told her I'd keep her in my prayers. She thanked me and then exited the car.

This trip reminds me of many others I've had as an Uber driver.

* * *

One night, I got a ding to pick up someone in West Mobile. He called me as soon as I accepted the ride. "I just had a fight with my wife. I'm about three doors up from my house, standing on the side of the road. I had to leave the house. It was a bad fight."

When he got in the car, he asked me to take him to a liquor store. He said, "We've been married a little over three years. We can't have kids, which adds to the tension."

Once he got the liquor, we pulled over and talked for a little while. "She gets so mad sometimes, she actually tries to choke me! My parents have been married for more than fifty years. I have lots of sisters, and my parents give the same advice to all of us. 'Never fail to go to bed together, even after a fight.'"

He didn't open the bottle and eventually asked me to drop him off a few doors from his house so he could think and settle down before he went back inside.

That was much easier than this next one.

* * *

I picked up a couple from the Bragg-Mitchell Home, a well-known venue for wedding receptions. I assumed that the couple was married as they got in the car. I found out very quickly that this was just their second date. She was disgusted with him, as he was major-league drunk.

He became increasingly obnoxious, so she moved to the right-hand side of the back seat. She asked him to stay on his side, then said, "Are you going to get sick?" That started all kinds of bells going off in my head. I offered him a throw-up bag and explained that it would cost them $150.00 if he got sick in my car and didn't use that bag. He tossed it back at me in the front seat. I made it clear to him that he was to stay on his side.

He began to cuss at her until I threatened to drop him off in the middle of the Bayway if he didn't calm down. Unfortunately, he sat directly behind me, so I couldn't see what he was doing. She was getting more and more scared and upset. From their conversation, I gathered that his vehicle was in her garage, meaning I needed to get them together so he could get his car and leave.

Her ex-husband was a former law officer and a 'friend' of this guy in my car. He was threatening her and me. "I'll get you sent to jail," he said to her. "And I'll have your license revoked, and you'll never drive again!" he told me.

We got to her house, and I told her to let him in, then come back and stand by my car on the street with me. She had texted friends who would be there within 10-15 minutes. He was not happy at all with this situation and kept cussing at us as we stood by the car.

This guy had trouble getting his car out of the garage, so I had to lift the garage door higher for him to leave. He was very agitated that I hadn't gone, but I didn't think he would leave if she had been alone. It seemed irresponsible to let him drive off drunk, but I decided that it would be better than exacerbating the current situation.

Once he left, she said, "I've never been more afraid in my life! Thank you for staying here!"

Her friends showed up a couple of minutes later. She shoved two bills into my hand and again thanked me. I told her she didn't have to do that, but I did appreciate the two twenties when I pulled them out of my pocket later.

I hoped she never saw that guy again.

* * *

One more quick story. This one combined tragedy and comedy all in one ride.

It was about 1:00 on Christmas Eve morning. I couldn't find the house, so I called the lady who requested the ride.

"You're about one house away. If you see a man carrying trash bags, that's him!"

I saw him standing by the side of the road with several trash bags.

"How're you doing?" I asked.

He answered, "It's a beautiful night for breaking up!" They had been arguing all night, and everything he had at her house was in trash bags. To add more confusion, he had recently broken his foot and was in a boot, hobbling around in the front yard.

He had left his kneeling scooter inside and returned to get it. This started a brand new round of yelling and screaming from his now 'former' girlfriend. He hurried to the car, jumped in, and told me to get him out of there! As bad as the situation seemed, he was laughing at the absurdity. She had an operation several months before, and they disagreed as to the mutual care each had given the other.

That was quite a contrast from all the other rides I had during Christmas. I would pick him up again a few months later. That's a story for another time!

Here is a little closing advice: Find someone you care about and give them a great big hug! It's much more fun to provide a ride for happy folks!

KICK IT UP A NOTCH!

There is often so much more to people than their outward appearance. Way more! One of the blessings I've received from ride-sharing is getting to know a little more about what's inside.

I picked up a young lady from a self-defense training business a while back. She told me that she owned the company, which she began because of an attempted rape against her during her youth. She was 8 years old when a 13-year-old tried to rape her. She remembers hitting him in the face with a metal toy car.

After that experience, her parents agreed to allow her to begin training in self-defense and martial arts. As she grew up, she traveled to Greece for additional training. Later, she trained with Israeli military personnel. I'd given her several rides over the last few months, and her stories always intrigued me.

She had kids and was raising them as a single, divorced mom. She seemed to have a generous heart, which had backfired a few times. Once, to help out a friend/acquaintance (not sure which), she took in a lady who needed a place to live. In a short time, she realized that this 'friend' had been stealing her child support checks and embezzled $300-$400 from her.

When she confronted her, the woman took a knife and threatened to commit suicide. Her training came into play. She was able to disarm the woman, and while she restrained her, she called her boyfriend and asked him to call the police and to come to her aid immediately. This was just one of the occasions she used her training in a real-life situation.

There is often an incongruity with some of my riders. Before I dropped the 'self-defense' specialist off on that trip, she asked me, "Would you mind dropping by a store and waiting just a minute for me? I need to pick up some shoes for a baby shower this afternoon. It won't take long, but it will save me a lot of time!" It's not the picture I had in my head.

Sometimes, it's the occupation or expertise of my riders that surprises me. For example, I picked up a very professional lady at the airport who would be testifying in a court case here locally. She had been a registered nurse in California hospitals and trauma centers for most of her career. Once, she was asked to testify in a murder case. The victim had been strangled. This happened maybe eight to ten years ago.

Attorneys asked her a few more times to testify in similar cases, so much so that she started her own consulting company, specifically as an expert witness. Specialization has increased in most professions, but I was still slightly taken aback when she described her two focus areas.

I asked, "What do you concentrate on the most?"

Her answer was, "Strangulation and Soft-Tissue Trauma!"

Now, she travels nationwide, specifically testifying regarding these two issues. I would have hoped that there wasn't enough of a market for that, but it seems she will be busy for the foreseeable future. Too bad.

"FINAL FOUR, AND ONE!"

This was around the time of COVID-19.

My car had never been cleaner! There was a bit of nostalgia involved. The experts say smell is the most powerful of all the senses. I believe that.

I was in Walgreens when I spotted it! One can left. One can of Lysol. No one was near it, so I hurried over and snatched it. I looked a little closer. *Cherry Blossoms and Pomegranate.* It didn't matter; it would kill 99.9% of all germs!

Here's where the nostalgia came in. I swear, my car smelled like the 1970s vintage of Boone's Farm Strawberry Hill Citrus Wine. My usual preparation for rides now included car washing, vacuuming, wiping down every square inch of the inside and the door handles outside, and finishing off with a healthy spray of Lysol on the seats and floor mats.

That week was probably the last week of ride-sharing for a while.

* * *

I received a ding after I prepped my vehicle and turned on my Uber and Lyft apps. I picked up a young lady who was carrying on a conversation on her phone. She waved and settled in the rear passenger-side seat.

She continued talking on her cell. "He's worthless, and he ain't gonna get any more chances. Girl, next time, there had better be 'Marry me!' in his talking. He's always on drugs or drunk. That's gotta stop!" The conversation went on like that for a while. Finally, I heard silence. At first, I wasn't sure if she was listening or if she had hung up.

She then told me, "You can turn your music back up. That was about my brother. He's in jail for about the fifth time. I don't know if he'll ever learn, but if he doesn't, he'll spend his life in there." I dropped her off and told her I'd pray for her and her family.

* * *

Next ding! I was in Prichard, 18 minutes away from my rider in downtown Mobile. There must not have been many drivers out because that's longer than usual. It was 'Frank' at The Garage, a casual bar just off Dauphin Street. I arrived, and it was packed. I called Frank and got no answer. I had to drive around the block and try again. A middle-aged man approached the car.

"Are you Frank?" I asked.

"What last name are you looking for?" he answered. (We didn't get anyone's last name.)

Two waitresses escorted him to the door on the passenger rear side. He didn't seem to be able to accomplish the walk on his own. He sat down, and the waitress helped him with his seat belt. The bar was 'celebrating' the last open night before closing due to the virus.

"Do you know where we're going?" he said. I gave him the address, and he nodded. "That's right. Do you know where that is? What is this? What are we in?"

I did my best to answer his mostly incoherent questions. Finally, we reached his home. I asked him if he needed help, and he declined. He stepped out, slammed the door, and fell against the front door. He recovered and stumbled up to his carport.

* * *

Another ding! This one was for the emergency entrance at Providence Hospital. More Lysol and wipes, then I was on my way. I pulled to the entrance, and a man wheeled a lady up to the passenger side.

"Can she sit up front, please?" he asked. She was a relatively large woman, so I agreed. He helped her in and said, "Love you, Mom. Take care."

The trip showed that we would be going about 17 miles away. She began to tell me her story. She was recovering from cervical cancer and had been having bladder problems. (Way more details than I needed to know, but way less than I would know by the end of the ride.) She continued talking, almost without taking a breath. She told me she arrived at the hospital this morning via ambulance.

"I begged my daughters and my son to take me, but they couldn't be bothered. Three of my daughters live in Mobile, and my son lives in Satsuma." In great detail, she described all of the procedures she had endured. We finally arrived at her house.

We pulled into a dirt driveway in the back. The place was a mess. She showed me something covered with a tarp next to a windmill without access to a breeze in months and told me that her mower was under that tarp. That kept it from being stolen. She was reluctant to leave the vehicle and continued to talk. I asked if she needed help to get inside. She said she could handle it. She needed prayers. I offered them to her.

* * *

Fourth ride. Ding! Another long way to go for the pickup. This time, a lady needed to go to Winn Dixie to pick up a few items. It was a round trip. On the way back, she told me to take a shortcut. We did. Then, we drove up to an intersection blocked by a stationary train. It was dark, and we couldn't see the end either way. We finally gave up and went back to the route suggested by the app. I dropped her off.

This was my last ride for the night. Unfortunately, the train was moving, and there was no escape route. I waited for the next 15-20 minutes until it passed. All of my passengers needed these rides. I tried to decide whether it was time to stop for a while.

The next night, I turned on my app. I got a request

immediately. I picked up a couple and took them to a BBQ place so they could have dinner. They would eat it outside, so this was not a round trip. They spent the time discussing whether it was time to buy a home. The fare for me was $3.00. I waited almost three more hours. No rides. The market made my decision. I was done until this coronavirus was gone.

These were challenging times for all of us, especially for my wife, Lane. She had to share our loft with me when I would typically have been driving. We were doing okay so far. We played Yahtzee, rode our bicycles, purchased two puzzles, and enjoyed watching all the folks running, walking, biking, and scootering in downtown Mobile. We enjoyed seeing the many instances of kindness, thoughtfulness, and even humor during this time. We would have even purchased a bottle of Boone's Farm Strawberry Hill Citrus Wine if there hadn't already been a run on it at the store! Oh, the memories!

We decided we would get through this. We had done it before for hurricanes and such, but this was a little different. I hope everyone reading this kept safe during that harsh time, kept their physical distance, and used that time to close the gap in their hearts.

Pray for each other, and know that you, all my readers, are in my prayers always!

"GOING HOME!"

I would often pick up patients from the local hospitals when their doctors discharged them. They didn't have anyone to pick them up and get them home. Circumstances, I'm sure. But, this time, it was even more troubling.

I waited at the discharge ramp longer than usual. I heard my rider before I saw her. She was not happy with the nurse escorting her.

"You need to get me outta here! I'm looking for Tommy! You're wasting my time!" she shouted. I could tell this was going to be a challenge.

"Tommy! Are you looking for Carmela?" she said. I opened the car door and watched as the nurse tried to help her into the car. My rider was in her early seventies but barely mobile, and the nurse struggled to move her into the vehicle.

"Don't touch me!" she told the nurse, "You don't even know me. You are grabbing me wrong!"

Once the nurse eventually got Carmela seated, I wondered how I would get her out of the car. That became even more challenging than I anticipated.

We had only traveled about a half-mile from the hospital when she said, "Call this number!" I put my phone on speaker and dialed the number she requested.

"I'm coming to your house. I have an Uber," she told the man.

"Why are you coming here?" he responded. "I'm not home."

"I need to go there. I'll leave after the thunderstorms." (Point of clarification: It wasn't raining, and there was no rain in the forecast.)

His answer was somewhat abrupt. "Woman, last time you

were there, you f***ed up everything. I don't need you coming!" He hung up.

"That was my husband," she said.

"Is there another place you want me to take you?" I asked. I was able to change the final address from my driver's app. After giving me the new address, she conversed as though we had long been friends. She told me about her church and how long she had been a member.

"What church do you attend?" she asked.

I told her I was Catholic and a parishioner at the Cathedral downtown.

"I've always wanted to be Catholic," she said.

We arrived at her house. Now, the real challenge. I worked at a nursing home, but unless she needed me to raise some money, I was not trained in moving the infirmed elderly. I had seen how she reacted to a nurse trained to maneuver patients.

Her house had three steps approaching the front door. I slowly helped her put her feet out of the car and on the ground. She was holding on to the door, but I couldn't see any way to help her up the sidewalk, much less up the three steps.

"Go up on the porch and get my crutches," she ordered.

Amidst the clutter on the front porch, I spotted the crutches. In fact, I spotted about eight pairs of crutches. When I reached Carmela, I realized the pair I grabbed differed in size by about two inches. I also noticed that they needed handles. None of the crutches had handles.

She and I tried to move her, but we weren't progressing. My phone was dinging for additional rides, but there was no way I could leave.

"I don't need to go up there anyway," she told me. "Go get my chair over there on the side of the house."

I brought an old wheelchair to her side.

"Brush off the seat. It's just dust. It won't hurt you!"

I rolled her up the sidewalk to the bottom of the steps. She told me her neighbors would be home soon, and they could get me inside. She assured me that two big guys do this for her often.

"Close your doors and come back over here to me," she said.

I walked over to her. She reached out to me, took my hand, thanked me, and started praying.

"Lord Jesus, take care of Tommy. Keep him safe when he drives at night. Take care of his family. Thank you for letting him take me home."

I asked her again if she would be alright. She assured me that she was okay. I'm always touched when someone with more challenges than I've ever known prays for me. Maybe one of the reasons I kept driving was more than the money. Perhaps I was constantly amazed by the people I was privileged to meet.

Keep my riders and me in your prayers. We need them!

(Note: I often talk about one of our residents at the Little Sisters of the Poor. Her name is Sarah Wilder. After more than 108 years on this earth, she left us for her place in heaven. May she rest in peace.)

CHAPTER 3
FAITH

THOUGHTS & PRAYERS

All of my stories have been related to my Uber driving experiences. This one will also be, but I want to combine it with my 'real' daytime career.

I was the development director for the Little Sisters of the Poor in Mobile, Alabama. I was there for almost ten years. If you combine that forty hours a week with the more than twenty hours a week driving for Uber, you can imagine how much of life I've witnessed.

The beauty of older adults and those who care for them changed my life forever. I shared stories with more than 18,000 riders over the past 8 years. My eyes are open to how much we all have in common.

Prayer at the Sacred Heart Residence is constant. The Little Sisters of the Poor spend countless hours each day asking for blessings from God, often invoking the saints' intercession. St. Joseph and St. Jeanne Jugan, their foundress, are two of the favorites. I'll touch on that a little later in this story.

You know how hard it is to avoid politics in today's world. I only bring it up here because of the public criticism of those who offer 'thoughts & prayers' in response to the tragedies and challenges of our fellow humans. Unfortunately, we can't always pitch in physically to help everyone for whom we pray. Here's the thing, though: we can help those within our reach. Maybe we are the answer to someone else's prayer.

Late one evening, I picked up an elderly gentleman standing in front of Mobile Infirmary, holding only a plastic grocery bag. He was going home after spending about three weeks in the hospital. He had thought he would be there for a few days when he had first checked in. His family all lived up north and had come to see him early in his stay.

However, when it was apparent that he would be staying longer, they had already returned home. 'Jim' lived in an apartment several miles away. He asked me to pray for him. As I was helping him to his upstairs unit, a neighbor came over and offered to keep an eye on him. Jim apologized for the appearance of his apartment before we opened the door.

When we entered, all he had was a chair in front of a television with no other furniture. Also, the TV was on. I had a feeling it may have been on for three weeks.

He said, "Thanks for your prayers!"

* * *

The Uber app buzzed. I picked up an unemployed, single mom who told me she had a 16-year-old and a 4-year-old daughter. Her eldest daughter had spent the last couple of weeks at Strickland Youth Center. She was now at home under house arrest.

The lady said, "My daughter is really a nice kid. She just hangs out with the wrong crowd. This is my first Uber ride and the first time I've been able to get anywhere away from home."

I told her I would keep her and her family in my prayers. She seemed very grateful.

* * *

I picked up three passengers from Felix's Restaurant who were passing through Mobile on their way to M. D. Anderson in Texas to visit a close relative suffering from Stage 4 Cancer. They were almost positive this would be their last time to see him alive.

This made me open up about the death of someone close I had witnessed. I had lost my sister in a car wreck back in 1977. We had a long talk about how my parents coped with that loss. We discussed our belief that, in reality, our time on earth is infinitesimal when compared to eternity. The idea was that we can handle almost anything if we keep that thought in mind.

When we reached their drop-off point, one of the ladies

told me, "The only reason we had even stopped in Mobile was because we had two flat tires. After all we've talked about, I realize how most of our troubles are tiny in the scheme of things."

Then, she continued, "Please keep us in your prayers. You and your family will certainly be in ours."

* * *

So now, to the Little Sisters of the Poor. I know that I'm not in the league with the prayer life of these amazing women. We process thousands of donations through my office each year. On our donor cards and forms, the Sisters offer to pray for the intentions of those donors. Hundreds of those cards ask for specific prayers for specific people in their lives.

The most common petitions are these:

"Please pray for recovery from illness for my family members or friends."

"Please pray for those family members and friends who have passed away and those who mourn them."

"Please pray for those who have lost their faith so they may return to a strong belief in God."

In addition to ministering to the elderly poor, these Little Sisters spend most of their waking hours in prayer and petitioning for everyone who asks. There may be no more important task that they accomplish. Please pray for them and their vocation.

I hope to tell you more about my experiences at Sacred Heart Residence in one of my stories. In today's cynical world, you should know that there is hope and love all around us. I see it every day!

This chapter may seem more serious than my past efforts. Maybe it was the season. Perhaps it's the feeling of gratitude for the blessings of family and friends. I surely know the ultimate sacrifice of Our Lord and how much he loves me and everyone else born in this world.

As it was Christmas when I wrote this account, I hope you will keep me and my family in your thoughts and prayers during the beautiful season. Please know that you are in mine!

MORALITY & MIND GAMES!

Driving for Uber or Lyft can seem straightforward. Pick up someone, give them a ride, drop them off. Simple, right?

It doesn't always work that way. These two rides show how complicated it can get.

Saturday, mid-afternoon, I got a 'ding' to pick up a gentleman on Halls Mill Rd., near Dauphin Island Parkway. When he got in the car, he said, "You're gonna get some good rides today! We're going to head over to Dawes Rd. (about 12 miles away). I left something there last night.

"When we get there, just wait in the car. I'll get it, then I need you to take me to Fairhope (about an hour away)."

We arrived at the first address, an empty, sparsely wooded lot. He jumped out of the car, ran to a grassy-covered area, reached into the brush, and put something in each pocket. He hurried back to the car, and we were off to Fairhope.

We spent the next 40 miles talking about sports, especially college football. I didn't ask what he had in his pocket, and he didn't volunteer any information. I was going crazy thinking about what he had in my car!

We arrived at the main intersection in downtown Fairhope, and he said, "You can let me out right here... Thanks again for the ride!" He left a generous tip on the app.

I'm sure this was some kind of drug deal, but I had no idea what I was supposed to do. Later, I discussed this with a police officer and then the public safety director in Mobile. Both agreed that it was probably indeed some kind of drug deal but that with no more than I had seen, there wasn't a lot they or I could do about it.

That was much easier than this next ride.

It was the Friday before the 4th of July. I drove to an apartment complex in West Mobile. A lady got in the car with her 8-year-old and a 3-month-old in a car seat. We were going to something called 'Foley School-Based Health Center.' I hoped my imagination was just running wild.

She said, "I need you to wait for me if you would. I will need to go in and get a quick procedure. I don't want to wait to see if I can get a ride back."

Some people might say that this was none of my business, but I was praying that I wasn't delivering this young lady to have an abortion. Instead, I told her my wife and I felt blessed with five children. Yes, we even felt that way through the tough times!

Her responses just made me feel more unnerved. "I don't know how I would handle any more children. I think it would be almost impossible," she said.

Finally, we arrived at the center, and she told me it would be just 15-20 minutes. I went to get something to drink, then parked about a block from the center, awaiting her call. I kept praying that she wasn't there for an abortion and asking God to intervene.

I tried to Google the place to find any information I could, but I was unsuccessful. I kept thinking that she wouldn't have to go all the way from Mobile, but she seemed to say she had been here before and was more comfortable. Furthermore, she had no one to leave her children with, so they had to come with her.

Thirty minutes later, she called for me to pick her up.

"The doctor wasn't there. The attending nurse was not authorized to perform the procedure or prescribe the medicine for me. So they said I'd have to come back next week."

She took my phone number and asked if I could bring her back when she got a new appointment. I prayed that God would provide me with the words if I were supposed to do something. However, we never reconnected.

I know the temptation is to 'mind your own business,' and I understand that sentiment. After all, my rider may not have intended anything along the lines of my concerns, but her conversation sure sounded that way.

TIME FOR A CHANGE!

There are no 'rhetorical' questions anymore...at least not for Uber drivers. A little over a year ago, I got a request to pick up a young man in front of an apartment complex. I drove to the front of the building. He was tattooed all over. That was the first thing you noticed.

As he entered the vehicle and settled into the front passenger seat, I asked, "How's your week going?"

It's a question I ask almost all of my passengers.

"I need you to pray for me," he said. "I was kicked out of my apartment two days ago after a fight with my girlfriend. The police said that I was to stay away from there permanently. I can stay here temporarily, but I don't have anywhere to go after a couple more days. I'm twenty-eight years old, but I feel way older. I've spent several years in prison for drugs and other problems."

He told me he reported monthly to his probation officer. He was technically still an inmate but was allowed to work. He had a job, and that's where he was going now—the only thing he had to hang on to right now. He told me that he wished someone would take a gun and blow his brains out right now. He did not feel close to anyone, and those with whom he had surrounded himself had not been a good influence.

He said, "I was in Las Vegas a few years back. An older guy took me under his wing and asked me to help him do some things.'" He pointed out that it wasn't the illicit 'relationship' that most people assumed. "We rode in his car to various places. He provided 'weed' and other drugs to me. One day, we were riding with a girl in the back seat when I got into an argument with the guy. The argument escalated into a full-blown fight while we were speeding down the highway. When we pulled over, the police arrived and threatened to take us both to jail. The girl just ran off. After we assured him that

72

neither of us would press charges, I was left alone on the road."

I tried to remember my situational training for Uber, but I couldn't recall this particular subject. I did try to stress the positive side of his current situation, especially that he had a job. At his age, there was plenty of time left to change his direction.

I talked about living one day at a time, one thing at a time. Solve today's challenge. Somehow, life finds the right way to go when we focus on the immediate battles. That kind of talk can sound patronizing, but I've seen it work firsthand.

We talked about where he wanted his life to go. He hoped to save money with his current job and then go to welding school. From there, he wanted to get a CDL and drive trucks. He had hope but was constantly overwhelmed by negative thoughts. I congratulated him on his plans but reminded him to work each day to be his best that day. He then told me he had applied for an apartment to have permanent residence.

"They asked on the application if they would find anything from a background check. I told them no. I hope they don't check that," he said.

We pulled up to the front of the mall. He looked at me again, "Please pray for me."

I responded, "Of course I will!"

I then realized he meant right now! I took his hand and hoped that I knew what to say. (Sometimes, Catholics are accused of only praying with pre-written, memorized prayers. I admit the temptation to do our ritual blessing before meals."Bless Us, O Lord, and these Thy gifts...")

I began by asking God to be with us at that moment and to lead him down a path of faith and service to Him. Immediately, my rider began sobbing uncontrollably. As tears flowed from his eyes, people continued to walk by my car. I finished praying, and we both sat in silence as he struggled to regain control of his emotions. He opened the door and started walking to his job.

I hoped for him to find a place to live. I hoped he put so much effort into his current job that he earned a great referral to a new career. I hoped he found his way to believe that God had a place for him and a path to follow. I hoped he learned to be a positive example to everyone he met.

Finally, I hope now you will include him in your prayers. It is time for a change!

THERE IS HOPE OUT THERE...SOMEWHERE!

You may get the impression that every rider (except you, of course) we ride-sharing folks pick up has some sort of addiction or behavior problems. Most don't, but they seem to make for interesting stories. Especially this one...

I got a 'ding' to pick up someone at the Mobile Airport. This was slightly different than usual because I wasn't near the airport. The app told me it would be a 'greater than 45 minutes' ride. (Uber told us that in case we weren't available for that time. Most of my fellow Uber drivers and I loved these rides.)

I pulled to the concourse and picked up a 'middle-aged' woman with a suitcase. She had ordered an 'XL,' which usually meant several passengers or a lot of luggage.

"How was your flight?" I asked.

"I was supposed to fly out, but my plans have changed. I need to ask you a favor. We're going to Brewton (about 90 miles away) to pick up my brother. He's being released from the Escambia County jail today. Here's the favor I need. When we pick him up, we need to go to Evergreen, Alabama, to the Greyhound Bus station."

"I'm more than happy to do that," I said.

She continued, "Once we drop him off, I need you to take me back to Mobile to a hotel. I just booked a room there and will fly out tomorrow. This whole situation has been crazy! He needs to get out of that jail. We were in court in Mobile today, and after our hearing, the judge released him, but for some reason, they needed to take him back to Brewton to release him from there."

Kate and her brother, Richard, were from Pittsburgh. She was in her early fifties, and he was in his late forties. During his twenties and thirties, he had stayed in trouble. He was hanging out with the wrong guys, abusing drugs and alcohol, and doing all of the associated activities. Interestingly, he had secured a job with the Correctional Department in Pennsylvania. He seemed well on the way to straightening out his life but still found his way to get involved with an addicted woman.

Because of Richard's challenges, Kate decided early on to become an addiction counselor. Her training and experience helped her identify the 'problem' woman who had become attached to Richard. Somehow, this other woman was involved with some unsavory characters who were involved in transporting narcotics to other states. It was one of these trips that Richard had offered to accompany this woman that rekindled his troubles.

Kate had flown to Mobile as an 'expert' witness. It seemed unusual for the sister to be an expert witness, but it worked out for them. I'm unsure of the details about Richard's trip with the other woman, but they were apparently pulled over and arrested. Someone had hidden narcotics throughout the vehicle. It seemed that he would have to atone for that mistake at some point, but in the meantime, he'd participated in the AA/NA program.

I was a little confused. How does that get him here in Mobile or Escambia County Detention Center? Somewhere along the way, he was required to take a drug test. He failed it, but just barely.

Word to the Wise: If you're doing the right things, **KEEP DETAILED RECORDS!!!**

This is where Kate's expert testimony came in. She told me, "Richard kept detailed records of everything he did under the 12-step program. Everything! Every meeting he attended, all the exercises he performed during his sobriety, everything you could imagine. As an expert in drug abuse therapy, I could see that he was doing the right things. There wasn't enough time to do otherwise. He lived with our family."

"Then, how did he fail the drug test?" I asked.

"Well," she said, "it was positive for opiates but well below the normal positive level. Richard's history caused them to react more aggressively than they would otherwise. We were amazed because we just knew he hadn't taken any drugs! Then it hit us. The night before the random drug test, my mother had served a salad dressing that contained poppy seeds. It wasn't on the front label, but it was one of the ingredients when we looked.

"We brought the bottle to court in Mobile, along with the receipt showing the purchase a day before he used the dressing. At first, the court seemed dubious, but the prosecutors even came aboard with all of the other testimony. We believe that evidence and lots of praying eventually convinced the court. Our family was raised Catholic, and even though Richard had strayed during his younger years, our faith has made a difference."

We then arrived at the jail. Somehow, Kate had checked the bus schedules and decided to take Richard back to Mobile with us. He would leave from Mobile in the morning on a 5:00 am Greyhound. They hugged in the parking lot and returned to my car.

Richard was deliriously happy. Apparently, the Escambia County facilities leave a lot to be desired. As we drove back, the conversation was lively. Even though they had been in court together earlier, the atmosphere seemed more like an overdue family reunion.

"All I could do since I've been at this jail and the whole time in court was to pray the 'Our Father' over and over," Richard said. "I tried to remember other prayers, but this one kept my mind focused."

"Well," Kate replied, "I was praying the 'Hail Mary' at the same time!"

I know that's what got us through this whole thing!

We had a great ride back to Mobile. Richard was aware that he would be spending some time in correctional facilities once he got back to Pittsburgh, but he seemed to accept that fact. I was touched to hear that he would serve that time but not let his temporary mistake affect the rest of his life. He had turned the corner and wanted to re-establish the practices he had learned from his faith and the 12-step program.

As I dropped them off at the hotel, I couldn't help but admire the support and encouragement he received from his sister and apparently from the rest of their family. Yep, I've added them to my prayer list!

"A PICTURE & A THOUSAND WORDS!"

"Jesus Christ!" shouted my passenger as he sat in the front seat to my right.

Even the other passengers stopped their conversations to find out what the outburst was all about.

"You have a picture of Jesus up here!!" he said. "That's pretty cool!"

Once we all realized he wasn't warning of some impending crash or earth-shattering event in view just outside of our windows, we gave a verbal sigh of relief.

"Why do you have that picture down there?"

The 3" x 5" picture sat on the console next to the gear shift.

"I have that picture there to remind me that no matter where I drive, He is with me," I explained. "This way, I always feel safe while I'm driving." My rider seemed to think that was cool. I had that picture there for almost three years.

I don't bring it up. It's really just there for me. It has sparked many discussions, though. I've been amazed at how it affects others. I've had more than ten thousand passengers in my car in the last three years. You can imagine some of the conversations and the colorful language my riders can use, especially late at night after abundant libations.

Back to the story, I got a kick out of a recent ride.

I picked up a group in their twenties. It was late Friday night, but these six folks were just beginning their pub crawl. Their evening obviously started somewhat earlier. The language from the back was slightly 'earthy.' I'm not a prude, but dang, could we possibly extend our use of the vocabulary to a little higher caliber?

The gentleman in the front seat with me glanced down at the picture of Jesus. He looked at me, then back at his companions.

"Hey!" he said. "Why don't y'all watch your language back there?"

"What's your problem?" someone yelled back.

"He's got a picture of Jesus up here. Show some respect!"

"Sorry..." he said to me.

It kinda worked like that sometimes. My grandfatherly appearance and white hair also seemed to help occasionally.

* * *

This next story is a little different, though.

It was late on a Monday night. I got pinged to pick up someone at a local bar. I saw a man's name on my Uber app, and I assumed he was the one hugging a lady at the door to the bar. She pushed him toward me and mouthed, "Thank you!"

The gentleman bounced back and forth between two cars as he approached. He chose the front seat.

"How's your evening going?" I asked.

"I hate those f***ing Jews," he spewed.

"That's too bad," I feebly responded.

After repeating himself, I thought about asking him to exit my vehicle.

"Don't you hate them?" he asks.

"I don't hate anyone," I said. "I don't have time for hate."

"You must not love our country." he continued.

I assured him that I loved my country. He asked me if I'd ever served. I told him I was an Air Force brat and that my dad had served for twenty years. He then shifted to a higher level.

"I bet you don't believe in God," he said.

At this point, I turned on my inside light, picked up my picture of Christ, and explained, "You see this picture. I not only believe in God, but He goes with me everywhere I go." This conversation had taken a turn I did not anticipate.

"You don't believe in Jesus. You just pretend. Let me see that picture." He paused. "You believe that Jesus is God?"

"I wouldn't make it through another day if I didn't," I told him.

He looked up at me, then back at the picture. Suddenly, the dam broke. Tears began to flow down his face.

"I'm so sorry!" he sobbed. "I'm so, so sorry..."

We continued the conversation for the next several minutes. He explained that he served overseas. He acknowledged that he believed in God and Jesus Christ.

"You believe that Jesus loves you? I know He doesn't love me. How could He? What do you know about Him?"

I told him, "I spend every day trying to learn more. But I know He loves me, and He is totally incapable of not loving you."

He continued to apologize to me over and over. I told him he had no problem with me, but I encouraged him to work on his relationship with God. We finally reached his house. He looked at the picture and broke down again. I had that picture in my car for almost three years then.

"Would you like to keep that picture?" I asked.

"Is that okay with you? Are you sure?" he said. He took a few minutes to calm himself, grabbed my hand, and thanked me.

There is no place for hate in our world. I'm often asked if I'm ever afraid when I'm driving. I'm not. This is not my average column. There was a time when I was afraid to be as open. I decided long ago that what other people think of me is none of my business. I know that some people are hurting in our world. I don't know why I didn't stop the car and let the guy find another way home. Maybe I was just supposed to be there at that moment.

I told this story to a friend of mine. He shared it with his girlfriend, who was raised by a Jewish father and a Catholic mother. Shortly after I told him, she gave him a package of cards with a picture of Jesus on the front. The picture was a print from a painting by her Catholic mother. The original is at St. Pius Catholic Grade School.

For this and so many other reasons, I'm grateful for the blessings I've been given. I just wanted y'all to know that you are a part of those blessings.

"CAUGHT SHORT!"

Sometimes, you need to make adjustments despite the best of intentions. The plan may look right, but the execution could be different.

Uber dinged me to pick up someone just off Old Shell Road. As soon as I turned the corner, I saw them. The couple appeared to be in their early 30s and sweating profusely.

"Thanks for showing up!" the young lady said. "My husband and I planned to run 3 miles, but we needed to stop halfway. We're a mile and a half from home."

Her husband slowly removed his hands from his knees and rose to a somewhat upright posture. His face was red, very, very red! "I thought 3 miles was shorter than this. I also thought I was in better shape."

They were caught short!

* * *

It was Senior Bowl time. I picked up a young man who was interning as a videographer for the NFL. They paid for his flight and hotel room for the week. I picked him up from the end of a street connected to a main thoroughfare. There was no house or business nearby, but he flagged me down.

"I just left the stadium at USA and started walking toward downtown, where the athletes are staying. I had to walk about 2-3 miles until my Uber app showed I could afford a ride. I can afford to go from here."

I asked him, "Why didn't you meet up with someone else who makes the same trip? I'm sure somebody would be happy to help."

"We've got a gathering tonight. I have almost no money to spend for the week, so I will have to find a friend!"

He was caught short!

I was driving in 100-degree, Mobile, Alabama temperatures. Uber dinged me to pick up a lady at a doctor's office. I noticed the office was closed but saw a woman in a nurse's outfit standing in front.

"Did they just close the office and leave you outside?" I asked.

"No, I work at another doctor's office a few miles away. I thought I could walk home since I was trying to save money. I started getting sick and knew I needed to Uber."

She was at least four miles from her home.

She was caught short!

* * *

It was dark, probably around 8:00 pm, and Uber notified me that I needed to pick up a woman in front of a nightclub on Hwy 90. When I arrived, I saw a woman standing on the grass between the lounge and a somewhat rundown motel. She had two large bags with her.

I placed the bags in the back.

"That's everything I own," she said. "I got kicked out of the motel. I was trying to get my father in Montgomery to pay for a week for me here, but they wouldn't accept his credit card on the phone.

"I was staying with my mom, but we got in a fight. She threw an ashtray at me, hit me in the head, and I had to get stitches. She's in jail right now."

The app said I was to take her to a discount store about five miles away.

"Where are you staying then?" I asked.

She said, "I'm gonna drop a few things off at the store. I work there. I tried to see if my manager would let me spend the night there after it closed, but she said we'd both get fired.

"I can walk to a ballpark to stay the night. I've slept there before, but I'm a little scared tonight. We're supposed to have heavy thunderstorms with lightning tonight."

I couldn't stand it any longer. I ended the ride on my app. "Is there any other place you know you could get a room for the night?" I asked. I looked at my Uber earnings on the app. $63.00 so far that night.

"The Taylor Motel told me on the phone that they charge $50.00, but I don't have enough."

"Don't worry; I'll cover a night there."

She began crying. "I'm going to be able to transfer to the Montgomery store and live with my father in a couple of weeks. He needs me to care for him, so it will work out for both of us."

We arrived at the Taylor Motel. I went to the window, you know, the kind with a hole to talk through and a slot barely thicker than a dollar bill on the bottom.

"I'm trying to help this lady with a room tonight. I understand you told her it's fifty dollars a night?"

He answered, "It's seventy."

I look around the motel. There was only one other 'guest.'

"C'mon, let's help her out."

"Sixty!"

I handed over my card. He gave my rider the key and a remote control for the TV.

She hugged me and told me that she was terrified of lightning. "I'm going to sleep so well tonight!"

So many people have helped me over the years when I've been caught short. I did have to explain to my wife, Lane, why there was a charge on my card for $60.00 to the Taylor Motel. She understood and agreed.

We couldn't allow this rider to be caught short in this case. I heard the thunderstorms rolling in late that night. I'm sure the rider slept better. I know I did. Please keep her in your prayers.

"PRAYERS AND PETITIONS!"

Uber gave me about eight or ten rides each weeknight to drive for them. If variety was the spice of life, ride-sharing gave me a full menu. This week, which I discuss below, was a perfect example.

Some of my riders have challenges in their lives. They tell people like me their stories because they don't think they'll ever see us again.

It was dark. I got a ding to pick up a lady in south Mobile. I asked her a question I often ask my riders. "How's your evening going?"

"My life is a mess! I'm going through the worst part of my life. I can't even remember when it was good," she said. "That's why you're taking me to the shelter."

"I'm so sorry to hear that," I told her. "What's going on?"

Through tears, she told me she didn't have anyone she could trust. "I've been yelled at, beaten, and told I'm not worth anything. I don't have anywhere to go other than the shelter. I need prayers. I've been trying to think about what God wants. I read and study, but I can't learn the answers."

We had to maneuver past a multi-car wreck, including ambulances and paramedics, to enter the shelter's parking lot. She did not get out of the car.

"Would you pray for me?" she asked.

"Of course I will!" I answered. "My men's group meets on Wednesday mornings. After 6:30 am Mass, we meet for an hour. At around 7:15 tomorrow morning, the Men of St. Joseph at St. Dominic Catholic Parish will pray for you.

"One more thing," I continued. "You're trying to learn your way to God using your brain. Before you go any further, open your heart. He'll be there. At least, that's the only way I know that works for me."

She thanked me, exited the car, and walked by another woman on the phone arguing with her 'significant other.' These ladies need our prayers.

* * *

Other riders need prayers for different reasons.

Later that evening, I got a call to pick up a lady at Walgreens on Government Blvd. The instructions told me to call the passenger upon my arrival. Just as I pulled into the parking lot, she called me.

"Where are you!" she shouted. "You should be at the front entrance, where the security guard is standing!"

I could not see a security guard.

"They're about to close! How come you can't see the guard!"

"I'm at the front entrance of Walgreens. I don't see a guard," I answered.

She exploded. "You're supposed to be on the beltline at Alabama Orthopaedic. Then you're going to take me to Walgreens to get my prescription, and then you're taking me home. You're in the wrong place!"

"You've put the pickups in the wrong order. You need to go on your app and change the pickup," I explained.

"I didn't put it in there! That nurse put it in wrong. You come to get me now. They're closing! You can fix it then yourself."

I told her I'd be there in about 12 minutes. When I arrived, I saw the guard. He was happy to open her door and help her into my vehicle. Too happy.

"Thank you for getting me. These people been messing me up all the time. They can't get nothing right. That GPS is always sending us miles away from where we're trying to go!"

Our conversation calmed down. She began telling me about her day. "God been so good to me. I been blessed. I been reading the Bible and doing my works. God sends good people to me. I got a mansion in heaven waitin' on me!"

She suddenly shifted the conversation. "You're not taking the interstate, are you? Most people don't know why interstates were originally built. I know!

"They built the interstates for trucks only. You got all these m@$#%!% $@^&$# cars $#%%^-ing up everybody out there. They should know better." She continued that line of thought for a few more minutes.

I was suppressing laughter, but not all that successfully. We arrived at the drive-up window at Walgreens. While we were waiting, she got a call. She was on speaker.

The voice said, "I'm Robert, your Uber driver. I'm at your pickup spot, but I don't see you."

"Robert, Thomas has already picked me up. You can get someone else."

When she hung up, she told me she's got three or four Ubers trying to pick her up. I asked her to cancel the others, or she'll get charged a fee.

"I'm not going to cancel; I'm scared I'll accidentally cancel you. God's been so good to me. The insurance is getting these rides for me. God's with me!"

"Yeah," I answered. "You've got God and four Uber drivers wandering all over the city trying to get you where you need to go."

When we reached her final destination, she asked me to keep her in my prayers. We included her in our men's group's intentions at 7:15 am. Our petition on her behalf was decidedly different from the shelter lady's.

"BLESSED!"

"Don't ask the question if you don't want the answer!"

I might not have asked the question if I had known the answer. Too late.

I picked up my rider at a car dealership. I started with my usual banter.

"How's your day going?"

"Not real good," she said.

Maybe I should have stopped there.

"So, what's going on?" I asked. Uber estimated that our ride would last about thirty-eight minutes, and I felt talkative.

"My car broke down. It's the kind that has a special key. They want me to pay $250.00 for a key and another $100.00 to find out why the car won't run.

"I was supposed to be taking a car home from there. I asked the dealership several times before I got an Uber to go there. They assured me that my credit was okay. Then, after waiting for at least an hour, they told me I needed a co-signer. I don't know anybody who can help me."

She continued, "None of my family is here. I don't have any friends who can help. I've got two kids and one on the way. My boyfriend is upset because now he doesn't have transportation to his job.

"I've been paying for my car for two-and-a-half years and still owe almost as much as when I bought it. I paid $10,000.00 for it and still owe $9,200.00."

"How much is it worth now?" I asked.

"They told me I could get about $1,500.00 for it."

"Can your boyfriend get his own car?"

"He can't drive," she said. "Well, he can drive. He can't get a license. He owes a lot of child support. The father of my oldest child doesn't pay child support. My husband, the father of my second child, died of COVID, and things have spiraled downhill ever since."

My head was spinning. I apologized, much too late, for intruding into her business. She told me she was happy to have had someone to talk to.

"People are much nicer here than where I'm from in Texas. I'm probably going to have to move back there with my mom. My boyfriend doesn't want to go."

(More intrusion on my part.)

"Maybe going there without him is not the worst thing you could do. What do you think?" I asked. "Do you get along with your mom?"

"We get along now, but our problems have always gotten worse when we've been in the same house. She offered to come get me and help with the new baby. I've thought about starting with her and trying to find my own place, but everything is too expensive. My brothers have apartments there, but they suggest I go to the 'cheap' area of town. The crime rate in those places is horrendous. I'd be scared for my children."

"What about other family or friends in other parts of the country?" I asked.

"My former mother-in-law has offered to take us in. Unfortunately, she blames me for the COVID death of her son. I also had COVID, and our child together had it. I applied for help from FEMA to bury my husband. They were supposed to give us $10,000. I found out later that she took the money and used it for gambling. When I told FEMA, they said she's the mother, and she had just as much right to it as I did."

She told me she had one more 'option.'

"My grandmother wants me to come live with her in Mexico. She's very sweet, but she's even been turned back by the cartel when she's tried to take a bus across the border. I don't want to bring my children up in such a scary area."

I should have shut up long ago, but now I was in too far.

"Do you belong to a church?" I asked her.

"No. I believe in God, but I don't see where he's been helpful lately."

I apologized again. "I'm sorry to get so personal, so feel free to tell me to shut up any time. Do you mind one more suggestion?"

She said she would love to hear anything that might help.

"There are people in churches who want to help. You need someone who will give you an ear and listen to your challenges. I am not telling you which church to approach. I'm very familiar with the work of Catholic Social Services in Mobile. Someone there will listen.

"You're still very young. You have a long life ahead of you and a chance to help your children. If you choose to move to Texas, reach out to Catholic Social Services there or ask around for other churches."

We reached her house. I told her my men's group would pray for her on Wednesday morning at our weekly meeting. She thanked me for the talk and promised to give God another try. "Maybe somebody at one of those places has some answers. I need something soon."

There's an old saying that if you put all your troubles on a table and everyone else put theirs on that table, you would almost always take your own back if given a choice.

My wife and I had dinner with long-time friends the night after this ride. We talked about good and bad times we've had during our lives, and we've both had our share.

I told my friend, the husband, about my rider. He paused, looked at me, and said, "You and I are blessed!"

I agree.

A CHRISTMAS FAVOR

I was in the rookie league after taking off some time ago. Until I reached 200 points again, Uber would not tell me how long the ride would last.

So far, all of my rides that day had been very short. Uber allowed me to set the direction for the ride search. I asked the app to send me toward home.

Ding!

Uber directed me to pick up 'April.'

April included directions, giving me a gate code. I didn't need the code. The gate swings opened on my approach. I also didn't need the description of the house. As I maneuvered down the long driveway, I could see kids, dogs, and a couple of ladies. I was unsure who my passenger(s) were until I saw one lady hugging the other and the children lining up for hugs.

One of the dogs was on my left, excoriating me for trespassing. I looked to my right and saw one of the children in tears as she waved goodbye to April.

"Good afternoon, April. Looks like they don't want you to leave!" I spoke. (I assumed she was an aunt or a close family friend.)

"Yes, that happens every time I leave," she said. "I miss them each time!"

My app told me our trip would last about twenty-five minutes.

She asked, "Are you from this area?"

I told her my story. Retired. Loved meeting new people. Wrote a weekly blog; most stories came from over 18,000 passengers in eight years.

"What kind of stories do you write?" she asked. I told her how to get to my website if she ever wanted to read some of them. She pulled up my site as we were talking.

I told her about a rider I picked up a few days ago. He was very wealthy and was involved in the family business. His parents were married for more than fifty years before their divorce.

April asked, "Do you get all your stories from when the riders are in your car, or do you follow up with them afterward?"

"With a few exceptions, I rarely see my passengers again." I then told her about an alcoholic that I drove about a dozen times. One of those rides included the man's son and a heartbreaking story from a Thanksgiving weekend for them.

She paused for a minute. "I guess I have a story also.

"Those children you saw back there are mine. My husband and I got involved in drugs several years ago. My mother is taking care of them while we go through separate, heavily-immersive rehab."

"Some states have a policy that allows family members to report parents to the authorities if they believe the children are at risk. It sounds unbelievable, but I've never been more grateful that my family intervened. My husband and I are about halfway through the six-month process, and we're both doing well.

"I live with six other women going through the same program. We use the 12-step Alcoholics Anonymous (AA) process. My life was a disaster, and I don't think I would ever recover if I weren't in this program."

She continued, "For me, the key factor is my faith. AA tells us to lean on a 'higher power,' which for me is God."

"I suspect that the higher power is God for everyone, even if they say they don't believe," I say. "Somewhere, behind all the denial, I don't see an alternative."

She agreed.

(Note: I spent five years on the board of directors for the Home of Grace for Women in my younger days. Each month, a resident would speak to our board members with a testimonial of her progress at the Home. During those years, many of us could recognize the addict's sincerity. Some of the ladies learned precisely the words they were supposed to speak. That experience caused me to believe in the sincerity and honesty of April's story.)

This challenge inspired April's mother, and she wanted to help addicts get the best treatment possible. My experience with the Home of Grace for Women showed me that many people with addiction and their families need much more intensive care than that provided by insurance. We were often the last resort after those folks had spent every penny available.

We discussed her hopes and dreams for a future with her family. I told her that I would pray for her and her family. I told her I belonged to a prayer group called the Men of St. Joseph, and even though I moved away from them in May, I would ask them to pray for her.

Christmas is a time for gifts. It's also the season for favors. I know some of the Men of St. Joseph members would read this story. Please add April to your prayers. And pray for April's mother and those who are desperately trying to help.

I'm asking for more favors. Please take a moment to pray for this family to get through this Christmas. Pray that the upcoming Christmas will be the best Christmas that April's family has ever had.

You have the power. So, do me this favor.

CHAPTER 4
HUMOR

LISTENING POST—
THE INVISIBLE MAN

I was driving around my usual Uber 'pick-up' spots, hoping to hear the familiar ding, signifying a ride request. So far—nothing. These dry periods allowed me to listen to podcasts, music, news/talk shows, and Sirius/XM comedy. Right now, it was comedy. I heard the comedian say something about Uber, which, of course, piqued my interest! He said, "Why do we open our personal lives, our most intimate feelings, to these random drivers? We never did that with taxi drivers!"

I didn't know why this happened either, but I suspected it was due to the feeling that someone was 'giving you a ride.' I can't tell you how often my passengers have begun or ended the ride with, "Thanks for picking me/us up!"

One example. I get a 'ding' to a local bar/restaurant known for its substantial wine menu. Once these five ladies entered my Santa Fe, we exchanged greetings, after which I disappeared into the background. Then, the ladies (fueled by the wine) began a deep discussion.

First, marital challenges (theirs), and then, the relationships of those not present. Then, the medical advice portion of the show.

"My anxiety medicine conflicts with my anti-depressant!"

"My doctor corrected that problem for me by adding another brand and changing the dosage."

"My friend says that splitting the dosage by taking half of the medicine in the morning and half in the afternoon will stop your problem."

I'm sure there is a substantial overlap between the marriage counseling stories and the anxiety/depression meds! Lots of prescriptions all around!

Eventually, 'Katie' began an intense discourse about her relationship with her parents. I knew her name was Katie because she had ordered the Uber and had her first name on the app. In the same way, she knew my first name was Tommy because that was on her app.

Katie relayed a story about her relationship with her dad and how much she desired his approval. Most of the ladies were in tears as she bared her soul.

Suddenly, one of the ladies interrupted to ask me, "What's your last name?"

"Fulton," I replied.

"Oh my gosh, I think my husband knows you!"

"What's your last name?" I asked. I recognized his name. We had worked together on a volunteer effort a few years back.

Suddenly, Katie said, "My dad says, 'Debbie, I'm so proud of your work, and, Debbie, you have really done well!'"

One of the other ladies interjected, "Who is Debbie? Why do you keep saying, Debbie?"

(She recognized my name and realized I probably knew her parents, which was true.) Now, I started dropping them off at different destinations. Katie was the first to reach her destination.

* * *

I want to pass on one lesson if I don't mention any others. (This is not the only time I've witnessed this, especially among groups of ladies. Guys can sometimes be as bad, but I have to admit, in my experience, women are more likely to experience this phenomenon.)

Never be the first in a group to leave the vehicle, if at all possible, especially after such a lively exchange!!! I'll leave it to you to figure out the consequences! (I promised to change the names and key details once they discovered my identity).

DADDY'S POOPED!

You know it's true. You are sure that your experiences are one-of-a-kind. Vacations, reunions, weddings, and funerals, whatever the reason, you retain memories because something out of the ordinary happens.

Ride-sharing has allowed me to experience some of those moments with my riders.

First, I ask for your indulgence in this story. This will be like those speakers I can't stand, who tell you to stand up, turn to the person on your right and left, shake hands, and tell them they are fantastic. I'm not too fond of that.

So, stand up and hold your hands in front of you. Shake your hands frantically as though you are trying to dry them without a towel or one of those hand blowers. Then, start moving your body as though dancing the 'chicken' dance combined with jogging vigorously. While combining all these gyrations, start screaming, "AAAAAAAHHHH!!!" as loudly as possible and run around in circles!

Okay, I know you're not really doing that, but I want you to put that in your memory bank. You'll need it later.

As the night began, I received my first 'ding' for the evening, just around the corner at the Shell Station. I entered the parking lot area and saw a young African-American family. The young man appeared to be about twenty-six years old, with two ladies standing beside him. I peeked into their car and saw a less-than-one-year-old baby sitting comfortably in a car seat.

The young man approached, "I bought this car three weeks ago, and it's caused nothing but trouble. I called the guy who sold it to me and told him I would not sue him if he would take the car back. He's keeping the down payment, but I'm not making any more payments.

"He's agreed, and we're waiting for the tow truck. We need a ride to the airport to rent a car. We came through Atlanta and spent a couple of days in Destin. I have to board a plane in Little Rock to start a new job in Wyoming. My flight leaves at 8:00 am tomorrow. I can't miss it. I will understand if you want to cancel the ride. I don't know when the wrecker will be here."

"No..." I said. "I'll be happy to wait. Let's go ahead and transfer everything to my car."

Once the luggage and other bags were aboard, it was time to put the baby and his car seat in my car. Those things have become way more complicated than when I was a new dad. I think my parents used the car seat when I was a baby, the same as everyone else in the car.

The ladies attached the seat and placed the baby gently beneath the straps. I wasn't sure which one was the mother, but neither seemed 'motherly' to me. The dad was on the phone planning strategy with the wrecker driver.

That's when it happened! The explosion was quiet, but the odor was unmistakable. What we witnessed in my cloth-covered seats was frightening! The baby must have saved up for days! Those fancy, disposable diapers were totally inadequate.

Closer inspection revealed that all the damage was contained within the confines of the baby seat. Dad quickly reached in, unhooked the car seat, and gently removed the occupant and seat together, placing them in an empty parking lot area.

This was the moment I realized that neither of the women were mothers. I say that because most moms I know are not surprised at anything by the time their baby is three months old. We looked at the young baby boy only to see that somehow, magically, he had managed to place a big clump of—well—it was square on the top of his head!?!

Remember the exercise I mentioned at the beginning of this story? Now is the time to bring that back into your frontal cortex.

The two 'non-mothers' were screaming to the top of their voices, dancing around the gas station, with a mix of emotions that combined horror and maniacal laughing. Of course, everyone nearby was deciding whether to duck for cover or run far away as fast as possible.

In time, the ladies successfully emptied approximately four or five boxes of baby wipes, cleaning the baby and every part of the car seat. They wrapped the baby's clothes in quadruple-bagged containers, and we were finally on our way.

I swear they should sell those white hazmat uniforms for this very occasion. Maybe I should keep one in my vehicle.

The drive to Little Rock was about eight hours. They should have arrived a few hours before his flight if everything went well.

The challenge didn't end there, though. When we arrived at the airport, the rental company turned down the young man. (Had they heard about the explosives this group was carrying?). No, he was trying to use a debit card to rent the car.

Luckily, he called his grandmother and could use her credit card to begin the last leg of their adventure.

By the way, those drugstore air fresheners really work. The memory takes a lot longer to dissipate.

THE VOTES ARE IN!

When you use the app to request an Uber ride, the driver only sees your first name. You only see the driver's first name. For most riders, this is more than adequate. This time, my rider introduced herself.

"Good afternoon, I'm Mary Maxwell. I'm the only woman running for the U. S. Senate in Alabama!" she proudly exclaimed. "I need to get my laptop repaired, and a nice gentleman entered the address on my phone for me. We'll be going to the Sam's Club at Springdale Mall. My campaign is at a standstill until I get this fixed."

That was in June 2017. Senator Jeff Sessions had been appointed Attorney General by President Trump. There were already ten candidates for the Republican nomination and several more on the Democrat ticket. In all honesty, I had never heard of this lady. The word 'eccentric' entered my mind.

Mary Maxwell explained, "I have lived in Australia for the last forty years. My husband, who was a native of Scotland, passed away in 2000. When we were married, he was a pediatrician in Adelaide, Australia."

She told me that she was born in New Hampshire and had run for the U. S. House of Representatives in 2005. For some reason, even though she had lived in Australia for the last forty years, she had been keeping up with politics in Alabama.

"To be a candidate for Senate in Alabama, I had to be a U. S. citizen, be at least thirty years old, and live in the state for at least one day. I intended to move to Montgomery, but when I got down here, someone had found a lovely place for me to live in Tuscaloosa, so I moved there instead.

"I've been traveling throughout Alabama by Greyhound and, of course, Uber. I'm still learning about today's technology, but I have always been active in politics. I once sued President Bush and Vice-President Cheney because they invaded Iran and Syria without congressional approval."

She then continued, "I have to say that for a lady from New Hampshire, I had never put much thought into Alabamians. I will admit that I've never been around nicer people. No one seems to be the least upset that some Northerner wants to be a senator here."

(Note: I think we're just mostly polite. Even though Ms. Maxwell was a lovely lady, it's probably not a great idea to replicate this campaign strategy in Alabama, or any other state for that matter.)

As we arrived at Sam's, she showed me the card from the gentleman who had agreed to fix her laptop. In the meantime, I received a request for a new rider, who happened to be at the same place. As she exited the front seat, a young African-American opened the back door and hopped in. At that moment, I noticed my former rider wandering around. The gentleman she was supposed to meet was in his shop a few miles away.

She hopped back into the front seat and asked if I could take her to the proper address.

I looked at the gentleman in the back seat. "Are you in a hurry? Do you mind if we take her first? I'll make sure your fare is adjusted so you won't have to pay anything extra," I asked.

"I'm not in any big hurry. I'll be happy to help!" he graciously replied.

Mary Maxwell continued her storytelling right where she left off. A few minutes later, we reached her destination.

"What in the world was that?" my newest passenger asked. Apparently, she sounded a little different to him also. He had the disadvantage of missing out on the story's beginning, told by a fascinating older woman with an Australian accent, combined with a Yankee twang, a brand new residence in

Alabama, and a desire to represent a state from the Deep South in the United States Senate.

"She wants to be your next United States Senator from Alabama!" I said.

"The show was well worth the extra ride time!" he laughed.

(Follow-up: Ms. Maxwell ran 7th in a field of ten Republicans, receiving 1,534 votes or 0.4% of the vote.)

MUSIC IN THE AIR!

Hey, Man! You got an 'aux' cord?

When I started driving for Uber, I read about the various things drivers should have on hand for their riders. An extra charging cord for iPhones and Androids, cold drinks, snacks, throw-up bags, and auxiliary cords so they can play their own music. I've found two of those things to be superfluous (snacks and drinks) and one that is to be <u>hidden</u> and <u>denied</u> to more than 90% of my riders.

I have a 4.98 rating out of 5. I stopped giving out drinks and snacks a long time ago. Here is what I've discovered after more than 4,100 rides. Show up on time. Be polite and respectful. Have a sense of humor. Deliver the passenger safely to their destination. It's that simple! (Although not often used, the throw-up bags have been my most valuable asset during some key moments!)

For the first six months, I tried to match my music playlists to my passenger's perceived tastes. That rarely worked. Then it happened!

Some young, excited, and inebriated college kids made the request. "How about some tunes?!?! You got an aux cord?"

I plugged it in and handed it to my rider. Big mistake! I am not a prude, but I heard profanity used in so many 'creative' ways for the next ten minutes. None of the songs stayed on for more than 30 seconds before someone else would tell my 'DJ' to change it. After a few more demonstrations on future rides, I somehow 'lost' (read 'hid') the aux cord.

Every once in a while, I give it another shot. A young woman asked if I had an aux cord so she could entertain the others in the car. "Sure," I said. "As long as it doesn't have the F-word in it."

She scrolled through her playlist. All the way down and all the way back up again. She had to have hundreds of songs on her list. "Never mind," she said. I can't believe we could listen to nothing on her list.

I have to confess, though. Music is significant to me. Not only while waiting for the magic 'ding' to tell me I have a new rider but also while watching the reaction to my playlists. I finally realized there was enough diversity in my music tastes to please 90% of my riders.

Even those folks in their twenties seemed to enjoy 'their parents" music, which was my genre—60s & 70s. I have a decent representation of the last several decades, surprising some younger crowd. "You like that song? I love that music!" they would remark.

Music has definitely played a part in some of my most memorable rides. One of those moments happened when I picked up an older African-American foursome, a gentleman and three ladies, at a restaurant on the Causeway. Simon and Garfunkel were playing on my radio. Bridge Over Troubled Water. The man started singing the song, and the ladies were accompanying him. I could not believe their voices. They were amazing. I wish the ride had lasted longer. I turned down the radio and listened to one more song by these folks before I had to drop them off.

There have been other times when it was just fun and just funny. Most of the young folks I drive are in the mood for partying. I had a large group of college kids in the car this time. I wasn't really paying attention to the music. Something playing on SiriusXM.

Then, this girl began singing a Bon Jovi song and told me she would forever remember this song as 'our song!' It was 'Livin On a Prayer.' One of the lines says something about Tommy and Gina. She was Gina. She leaned forward and blasted in my ear, with all the others singing along.

Another time, I picked up a 'thirty-something' couple from a bar downtown. We had a pleasant conversation when 'Bye-Bye Miss American Pie' came on the playlist. She knew every lyric of that very long song and sang it to the top of her voice!

Her husband laughed and said, "That happens every time that song comes on!"

We were nearing the end of the ride, at about 1:30 am, when she said, "Please, please play that one more time...I promise you'll get a great tip!" Her husband stepped out of the car and patiently listened to her belt out the music. I was glad none of their neighbors called the police!

The latest 'music' ride happened recently. Several minutes away from the airport, I was 'dinged' to pick up some passengers. When I pulled up, three young men were waiting, one strumming a guitar. As we drove toward downtown, I heard them discussing strategies for building and growing their band. I asked them the name of their band, to which they answered, "The Fab Four."

"I've seen you in concert twice in Mobile! I would love to have seen you again, but we're going out of town this weekend. So, which ones are you?"

The guy in the front seat said, "I'm George Harrison, and the guy behind me is Ringo Starr. Paul McCartney and John Lennon were in the car ahead of us."

The other guy was a member of the new group they were forming. If you ever get the opportunity to see The Fab Four, I highly recommend their show. I am still amazed at how you see the Beatles grow from their beginning through all the changes in their music.

As we rode into town, George and I had a great conversation. I told him I was an author, and he seemed genuinely interested in getting a copy of my book, 'An Act of Congress.' When we pulled up to their hotel, I gave him a copy of the book. He told me he was a 'believer' and asked me to sign the book. He had seen the picture of Jesus that I kept in the center console of my car and made it clear to me that faith was an essential part of his life. After all, George composed the song '*My Sweet Lord.*'

"WHAT SHE SAID!"

I wish I understood foreign languages. Many of my riders are from foreign countries, and most of them speak some version of English. Even though I've spent a little time on Duolingo trying to learn Spanish, I am at a complete loss regarding conversation.

I can hear a random Spanish word that I recognize, but I have zero ability to place it in context. Occasionally, I will thank my passenger with a "Gracias, amigo!" I'll probably stop doing that because of how trite and stupid it seems now that I've written it here.

The foreign tongue I come closest to knowing came from being an altar boy over 55 years ago, boosted by Latin I and Latin II classes in high school. The two most common phrases I've used since, outside of Catholic Masses, are not all that useful. 'Veni, Vidi, Vici,' meaning 'I came, I saw, and I conquered,' and 'Audemus Jura Nostra Defendere,' which means 'We Dare Defend Our Rights.' The latter is the motto for the State of Alabama.

One Friday night, I got dinged to pick up someone at a Cajun food establishment on Airport Boulevard. The name was Tiffany. As I arrived, 'Tiffany' asked me to wait a minute so she could get my passenger. I gathered that Tiffany was one of the proprietors.

"Do you know where you're going with my aunt?" she asked me. Hers was not a Cajun accent. More likely, the accent was of one of the 'ese' regions of the Far East, such as Japanese, Chinese, or Taiwanese. Regardless, I needed help understanding her destination wording.

"The Uber app says we're going to Mt. Vernon, about 52 minutes away," I answered.

The older lady and I began our trip. "How's your day going?" I asked.

"I'm OK," she answered. Then she said something about making a phone call. (Note: Sometimes, when a passenger is a little nervous, they will call someone to remain in contact. And, sometimes, they want to use the time to catch up on things.)

I want to say that I raised the glass partition between the front and back seats so she could speak privately, but I don't have such a partition. Besides, these conversations provide ride-share drivers with hours of entertainment and blog material for this particular driver.

As it turned out, I would only be successful at eavesdropping if I had spent hundreds of hours studying her language. Nevertheless, her words were very entertaining, in a musical sort of way!

"Tang don wak a teak doe wing do shishi!" she said. "Tok tak ding ding sow Mississippi doe bee tea lato." The high pitch was exhilarating! Hearing the tongue clicking against the roof of her mouth was just plain fun.

She continued, "I'm OK! Te twee wak wok tutilay da tang lee lee lan Mississippi. Hahahahahaha. Ha Ha!" I love to hear people laugh! Laughing and crying are two expressions of language that translate in every society.

Before she hung up on this caller, she laughed several times and said, "I'm OK" several times.

After she hung up, I asked her if the temperature was good for her in the car.

"I'm OK!" she said. Then, she made another phone call. This time, she was on speaker. I could hear both sides now. But it was just an echo of the same language.

You may have already recognized a familiar word in the conversations above. Mississippi. I guess states and cities don't translate into different pronunciations because I heard Mississippi, Austin, Honolulu, Hawaii, and other locations sprinkled throughout the discussions.

We approached our destination somewhere in the Mt. Vernon area. The roads got smaller and smaller until we turned off to a gated wooded area. It was very dark. No streetlights or other visible homes.

I had my bright lights on. I couldn't read the sign next to the open gate as we entered, but this seemed like something other than a residential neighborhood. Then, through the woods, I saw some lights. Lots of lights! We were approaching what appeared to be some version of a campground. We passed dozens of parked cars with lights on both sides.

Then, I saw groups of people walking around in Buddhist monk clothing. Several 'oriental-style' buildings were on my right, with a lake and pavilion to my left. I seemed to have stepped (driven) into another land. The view was beautiful but surreal.

"Where do you want me to drop you off?" I asked.

"Do you see the Buddha woman just ahead?" she replied. "I don't have any small bills for your tip. Do you have any change?"

I didn't, but she said she would let her niece know so she could tip me. I no sooner turned the car around than my phone app notified me of a nice tip. I fully understood that language.

Once I reached the main road, I turned around to view the sign at the entrance. It read, 'Tu Vien Lien Tri.' There was a Buddhist flag flying next to the gate. It turned out that it was a Vietnamese Monastery that held retreats and taught yoga. I had to try some of that Vietnamese/Cajun fusion food soon!

As I drove home from this hidden treasure, I could only think of two words from my high school Latin classes. 'Veni' and 'Vidi.' I have a lot of life to live before I can exclaim, 'Vici!'

"OVERRATED!"

Have you been rated recently? Have you rated anyone? Frankly, it's gotten way out of hand! They say that opinions are like noses; everybody has one. However, our culture has decided that we need to smell everything and let everyone else know what we think.

Uber asks its riders to rate the drivers after every ride. When you see a driver's rating, you see a compilation of your last 500 rides. Until recently, my rating for the last several months was a perfect 5.0. Then it happened! Somebody decided to rank me as #1! At least, that's my assumption. Surely, they couldn't have intended to give me a '1' rating.

Now, my rating is 4.99. And, of course, I have no idea what caused the low rating. Last year, someone actually gave feedback.

"He talked too much!" (Is that a real thing? Well, I never!)

Most riders are unaware that we also rate you. We must rate you and inform Uber of your seat belt use. You have to really mess up to get anything lower than five stars from me. After more than 9,000 rides, I've given fewer than ten riders less than five stars.

Frankly, we have gone massively overboard at quantifying our judgment of our fellow humans. It's everywhere!

My friends and I frequent a local establishment for our weekly gatherings. You can order food from several vendors and alcohol from a separate bar in the same facility. More than once, I've been asked to rate my service before I've received my order. I don't blame the folks working there; the survey is built into the software.

You cannot access anyone on the phone or online without receiving a 'short, two-minute survey' request from the service provider, which their IT and marketing folks designed to improve their service.

Not only do they ask that you rate them on a 'satisfaction' scale, but you are then required to provide a reason for your answer.

I'm not saying that we shouldn't take the time to evaluate consequential moments in our lives. Your potential spouse. Your job/career. Football coaches. Pizza toppings. You know— important things!

Another essential consideration is context. Maybe if we knew more about the subject we're judging, we wouldn't be so quick to rate.

* * *

I picked up a couple from one of the restaurants on the Causeway one evening. There was plenty of space for me to reach the other side of the highway and take a left before an oncoming car arrived. Suddenly, a car doing at least 80 mph came barrelling out from behind the visible vehicle. The lady in the back seat screamed at a decibel level comparable to a tornado siren.

"Kick it!" her husband yelled.

I did. We miraculously avoided the speeder and then outmaneuvered the merging traffic. Once we settled down, I joked, "Is this going to affect my rating?"

"Affect it?! You earned the biggest five stars I can imagine! We're still alive!" he said.

"I saw my life pass before my eyes! I thought we were going to die!" said his wife.

I don't know if I got five stars, but I did get a nice tip!

That's what I like! Honest feedback in real-time.

What bothers me the most about all these surveys is that computers conduct most of them. The same happens when you try to contact customer service with a question.

First, you have to determine the reason for your call from a long list of reasons, none matching the reason for your call. I know I'm not the only one who has resorted to screaming, "Help!" "I want a human!" "Operator!" "Agent!"

Cursing does not speed up the process.

Once you finally reach a human, if you ever do, you're exhausted. Whether they solve your problem or not, you will inevitably be asked to stay on the line to give your opinion of the service you've been afforded. Want to know my feelings? See the previous paragraph and add some expletives!

* * *

I have another reason for my dislike of rating systems. One of my recent Uber passengers is the perfect example.

I'd picked her up several times before. Usually, she was relaxed and glad to be getting off work. This time, it seemed a little earlier for her than usual.

"How's your day been?" I asked. "Ready to get home and relax, I'm sure."

She looked up from her phone. "What? What did you say?" she answered curtly. "Fine, I'm fine!"

Hmmm. Not as relaxed as usual. She was not in her usual talkative mood. So, it was quiet time.

Uber will sometimes decide to get creative with the routing. I took the new GPS route suggestion, which was a bad move.

"Hey, you're taking the wrong road," she said. I immediately corrected my route.

We arrived at her apartment complex to see paramedics and a fire engine in the parking lot. They were parked right outside her place. She got out, said something to one of the firefighters, and walked away.

I took a wrong turn on the way to her apartment. She was unpleasant and rude as a rider. I don't know how she rated me, but I gave her five stars. And prayers for whatever challenge she faced that night.

That's what I think about ratings.

"IS IT JUST ME?"

Or are we all suffering from a massive identity crisis? Again, I can't be the only one affected by all the new, wondrous security technology innovations. I swear I remember the days when you could push the 'on' button on your contraption and begin using it at once. (Well, that was an electric typewriter in Coach Radka's high school typing class at McGill Institute more than fifty years ago.)

I know some tech-savvy folks will respond with all kinds of remedies, but that's not the point. We now must use multiple devices to access one desired device.

It starts with my daily computer access attempt. I push the on button, and it begins. Computer password. Done. Then, several programs start to emerge.

Some program I never asked for, 'Team,' wants to know if I'd like to share my experiences with other team members. Then, Norton wants me to access a plethora of protection options. For example, Norton would like to access my camera. I don't have my camera on, but yeah, sure, go to town.

Next, Microsoft tells me that I now have a new code that allows me to bypass dozens of other codes, which should make my process more manageable. Except, it doesn't. Or I don't understand how to use it properly. So, I close that one.

To gain access to MailChimp, the program I use to distribute and evaluate these weekly blogs, I have to use a program/app on my phone that generates a random six-digit code. I'm now supposed to put my forefinger on the magic spot on my Apple SE iPhone and open the 'Authy' app. I have a maximum of thirty seconds to transfer that code.

Next, I open a Word document and begin typing my blog. But first, Facebook beckons, so I open it. The next thing I notice is an email that tells me someone has tried to access my Facebook page from an unrecognized source. I'd only logged into Facebook from three different devices, none of which Facebook ever recognizes.

The tech folks have tried to help us. When I don't remember a password or username, I can simply hit Google, Facebook, or another program I might use repetitively enough to recall. However, it doesn't end there.

The next instruction is to open my Gmail app on my iPhone 5 or iPhone 23. It's the same phone, but some cloud person decides to renumber my phone each time.

Then, the app opens and says, "Are you trying to sign in?"

I answer, "Yes, it's me."

Just one more thing before I tie all this back to Ubering. Do you ever see the prompt that says, "If you press here, you won't be asked to enter all that other stuff for at least two weeks?" It never works. I'm asked to enter all that other stuff every time I open the program.

So, Uber.

A couple of weeks ago, after a full day of work at the Little Sisters of the Poor, I began my usual ride-share routine. My first request was to pick up someone on the south side of Government Street. I arrived at the designated address and received a text from my passenger.

"I'm at the hospital's discharge door."

I was not, so I called her. "The app says you're at a home address. Did you accidentally put in the destination rather than the pickup? I asked.

"No," she said. "I don't even recognize that address."

We tried to reroute it but finally gave up.

* * *

A few rides later, I was assigned to pick up Aaron at an apartment complex. I received a phone call as Aaron was approaching my car. I lowered the window as Aaron waited outside the vehicle. It was Uber. The call was on speakerphone.

"I'm required to inform you that you will have to discontinue driving at once. We received multiple complaints that your picture doesn't match your face. Also, three riders say that you were swerving."

"That can't possibly be true," I protested. "I've been driving for more than seven years, and I've never had a problem with my face. My rating is 4.99, and I've never had a complaint about swerving. My rider is standing here, and I'm going to give him a ride."

Uber responded, "I see that you have a rider. I am informing you that you must stop driving as soon as you reach the destination. We will be contacting you then."

Aaron said, "I'm looking at your face on the app, and you are a spitting image."

As I was driving, we were both amused by the call. On the way, I received another ding to pick up a rider. So much for Uber cutting me off. Aaron gave me a wonderful tip.

* * *

I'd now picked up 'Skye.' As promised, Uber called me back. "We've had more complaints. Five riders have reported that your face is not the one on the app. And four riders have complained about your swerving!"

Skye agreed with me; my face was unerringly similar to the app version. I argued with the Uber guy about how crazy this was. He apparently agreed because he hung up.

* * *

For my final ride, I picked up four students from India who were attending the USA. I told them the story. The young lady sitting up front, looked at the app, looked at me, and said, "Well, I do see a difference in the picture and the live you. In person, I think you have more chins than the picture shows. But that could just be the angle."

Oh, but aren't these young folks humorous nowadays? Probably tech majors!

"LOCATION, LOCATION, LOCATION!"

Where are we? You would think that with GPS and all the hi-fallutin' high-tech out there, we'd never get lost. One of the things people assume about Uber drivers is that we learn every square mile of our territory. However, technology has replaced the need to store that knowledge in our brains.

So, here's what happened. I got a ding to pick up a rider. The app showed a map and a white line I was supposed to follow to reach my pickup point. I was pretty sure the phrase, "Can't see the forest for the trees," applied here. Occasionally, I'd click on the destination to get an idea of what part of town I was targeting.

* * *

Sometimes, the driving directions didn't account for the driving conditions. I dropped off a student on the USA campus one night. The GPS told me the exact directions to leave campus and head toward my next pickup. Meanwhile, the police had closed off every known exit to accommodate a nighttime 5K race.

The traffic cops sent me back and forth several times across the campus, insisting I could exit through the other side. Eventually, they let me leave through a gap in the runners. GPS had no idea.

I'd discovered one gigantic satellite-free zone throughout my seven-plus years of driving. A few years ago, I disappeared from view near Leakesville, Mississippi. I was taking a fascinating gentleman from Mobile Airport to an off-road race there. Somewhere about twenty minutes from our destination, we disappeared from the app. Also, I had zero phone connection.

I wrote a story about this ride called '*Rednecks with Paychecks!* The ride included two near misses with deer on the way and another close call after the drop-off.

My only clue for direction was the compass on my mirror. I knew Mississippi was west of Alabama, so I headed easterly according to my mirror. Following the road, my mirror slowly changed to the northeast, then north. Even though I saw a road sign that said I was heading toward Alabama, I would cross the line far north of my ideal re-entry point.

I turned around in a driveway. That's when the third deer jumped over the front end of my car. Eventually, one-fourth of my phone screen began to display my map. Technology returned, and I found my way back home.

I miss the days when I could pull out my origami-folded map and plot my directions.

None of my experiences during my Uber driving matched my foray into the 'Twilight Zone,' better known as Hillsdale Heights. For those of you who are unfamiliar with the neighborhood, it was once a thriving community, which later became off-campus housing for many USA students before degenerating into a crime-ridden, drug-infested area.

* * *

One evening, I received a rider request after dropping off some students on campus. Somehow, the GPS routed me through the long-abandoned Hillsdale Heights neighborhood. I hadn't been in that area for decades, mainly because it had been closed off. Someone must have removed a barricade.

The roads were still there, but there were no homes or streetlights. There were still driveways that ended short of where there used to be residences. Every exit I could find was blocked by impassable barricades or high mounds of dirt.

My GPS still showed the roads but not the barricades. I was becoming a little desperate as I searched for the spot I had entered the neighborhood. I know I didn't jump a barricade, but the more I drove, the more confused I became.

My mind began to play tricks, and I started imagining

college parties hosted by ghosts decades ago. The only pieces missing were the houses and the people. Very eerie.

I called my rider and explained that I was heading toward him. I didn't want to explain that I had fallen through some time warp and would need to regain my sanity first. Riders tend to get nervous with that type of excuse.

Suddenly, I saw the unblocked exit that had originally delivered me into this nightmare. I was again free to pick up folks I'd never met, only to transport them to places I'd never been. Besides, I could carry on a meaningful conversation, eavesdrop on my riders, or memorize our routes. I preferred the first two options.

Big-city taxi drivers would sooner die than admit the need for artificial intelligence to guide their travel. I was still depending on the white line on my Uber app.

I'd read somewhere recently that we don't exercise our minds as much as we used to. We have access to more information than ever, but we don't store it because we can 'google' everything we need to find out.

More than seven years after beginning my Uber driving adventure, I sometimes became more confused than ever about my location. Some nights, I might start driving in Prichard, Creola, Theodore, Grand Bay, all over Baldwin County, and who knows where else.

More than once, I've had to ask my car's GPS to tell me how to get home at the end of a long night. Too much dependence on tech? Probably.

I've been in every nook and cranny in Mobile and Baldwin counties. Just don't ask me how I got there.

"DELUSIONAL HAPPINESS!"

Uber beckons! I would reach my pickup point, board the rider or riders, and give my usual greeting, "Happy Tuesday!" or whatever day of the week is appropriate. Most riders would chuckle and return the wishes.

Sometimes, they'd question my enthusiasm.

"I'm always happy!" I would explain. Then, I'd pause and follow up with, "Of course, I'm delusional, so I only have to convince myself."

Some people can't stand that attitude. I get that, too. But you might as well start off the ride in a good mood.

Several years ago, I picked up a gentleman downtown who needed a ride to the University of South Alabama's Mitchell Center. He was a nice guy!

When I asked him what brought him to Mobile, he said he was performing at the USA campus with Marlon Wayans. I asked his name. I thought he said his name was Jay McFerrin.

"Oh yeah," I said. "Don't Worry, Be Happy! I love that song!"

"That's Bobby McFerrin. I'm a comedian! You may have heard me on some of the comedy channels on SiriusXM," he said.

I only listened to two comedy channels. I tried to fake it, but I'd never heard of him. Then, he told me he played Dr. Carson on Saturday Night Lives take on the 2016 Presidential Debates. I remembered his role in those sketches. We were both relieved that I now had some point of reference.

I wanted to look him up later, so I asked the spelling of his name.

"J-a-y P-h-a-r-o-a-h," he said.

I made some flimsy excuses about the spelling being why I

didn't recognize him.

I was looking for a way to redeem myself when I realized where I was. Crichton! The Leprechaun!

"We're currently located in one of the most famous areas in Mobile. Have you ever heard of the famous Leprechaun?" I asked.

"You mean, 'Where da gold at?'" he replied. "That is one of the funniest things I've ever seen. I remember it well!"

"Are we in the hood?" he then asked.

We laughed as he assembled a few lines for that evening's performance. I mentioned we would travel through one of the more upscale neighborhoods before reaching USA. I don't know if he ever used the story.

Mr. Pharoah, Jay, as I like to call him, made folks happy professionally. Or, at least, he made them laugh.

* * *

Sometimes, riders challenge my attempt at maintaining a happy atmosphere. A week after that, I picked up a couple who seemed in a good mood. Then it started. A remark here, a retort there, and the disposition changed.

We dropped off the young lady and proceeded to the gentleman's destination.

"#*%∧∧&," he said. "I forgot my charger. We gotta go back!"

It was hard to believe these two were ever amicable when we retrieved his charger. I was playing some light, happy tunes on my radio. He said nothing but began to turn the volume up on his phone. I eventually turned my music off. Now, I had lost my happy mood as the lyrics from his music (?) got increasingly graphically filthy and hateful.

I admit to regaining my good mood almost immediately after dropping him off. Happy again!

Sometimes, you get a surprise from a rider. The world seems a lot smaller.

I picked up a young lady in south Mobile County. I love it when my passenger answers my "How's your day going?" question with something more than "Fine" or "OK." Her answer was one of the more descriptive.

"It's been an exhausting day. I've got an autistic son, and some days can be a challenge. But it's much better than it used to be. He tends to be a loner and doesn't interact well with other kids. He is in a Special Education program at his high school."

"My brother-in-law teaches Special Ed students in high school," I mentioned.

She suddenly got excited. "Is his name Ray Young?"

"Yep!" I replied.

"He's wonderful! He took the time to sit down with my son and teach him how to do something on his iPad, which has made a world of difference in our lives."

Now we were both happy! Ray had a love for those kids and the perfect temperament. My son-in-law worked with the same challenged kids at his high school in Franklin, Tennessee. Several of my kids and grandchildren had volunteered to help add joy to the lives of these young people. The joy came back ten times!

* * *

A good friend, Jerry Taff, told me a story that day that might explain this story. He retired a few years ago after a successful career in the financial services industry. He worked as a substitute teacher in Montgomery.

He worked with the younger grades and loved being around those kids. He and his wife were expecting their first grandchild. Jerry's other daughter taught first grade at the same school. She and Jerry decided to let Jerry tell the students that their teacher would be an aunt. They cheered.

Then, Jerry asked the kids a follow-up question.

"If your teacher, my daughter, is going to be the aunt, what does that make me?"

One enthusiastic little girl waved her hand in the air. "I know, I know!"

She stood and proudly answered.

"Happy!"

And the grandfather-to-be agreed wholeheartedly!

CHAPTER 5
LIFE BALANCE

TESLA TIME!

You have no idea who you will be meeting as the 'ding' hits the Uber app. This particular ride was one of my most memorable and favorite rides.

8:00 pm on a Friday: Uber summoned me to Sam's Club. They were traveling through Mobile on their way home to Houston. Their accents were most assuredly not Texan. Robert was from South Africa, and Abi was from Great Britain.

They had left Destin earlier that day with a new prize. They had purchased/won a 2010 Tesla in a charity auction, which raised more than $3,000.000.00 for 12 different charities. Their package included wine, a week-long trip to some resort, and a Tesla.

Unfortunately, when they arrived in Mobile, they discovered that their charging cord did not match the more updated charging stations at Target. After calling all over the place to find a remedy, someone at Tesla advised them to order a new charging cord that would arrive a few days later.

Tesla reps told them another alternative was to find a trailer park, which should be equipped with older equipment. That's where their car was now. He told me two stories about his previous Uber experiences on the way there. On one occasion, the driver had to track him down to return his wallet. The second time, it was his keys.

"Y'all seem fairly high maintenance," I joked.

"Just wait and see," he responded.

It was the definitive picture of incongruity! Parked next to the Tesla sports car was a 1970s vintage (my guess) Winnebago. Robert asked me to wait while he met with 'Taz,' the somewhat earlier vintage RV owner. Wearing a slightly aged Alabama Crimson Tide cap, Taz welcomed him into his home.

Taz informed Robert that the breaker kept popping,

meaning the Tesla had only charged enough to last about six minutes. The last six hours had been a total waste.

Robert asked me, "Would you mind driving us to New Orleans right now? We have to be back in Houston right away."

"I'll be happy to do that," I said.

The drive to New Orleans was great. He told me about his work in the oil & gas business. I discussed my work with the Little Sisters of the Poor, and he handed me two twenties to give to the nuns for their work. It was a nice gesture!

He had also started a new business with his daughter, which was similar to the more well-known 'Blue Apron' operation. They delivered pre-packaged healthy meals to their customer's homes.

Abi had started a charitable organization to provide the homeless with a week's clothing. These were genuinely lovely people.

When we reached their hotel in New Orleans, I asked them if I could help with the car. They sent a car carrier to pick it up and transport it to Houston.

He handed me three twenties and the keys to the Tesla. "We'd like you to meet with Taz on Tuesday to ensure the car gets loaded properly. They need someone to sign off on the condition of the car. If you and your wife are ever in Houston, we'd love to put you up in our place!"

That Tuesday, I had a great conversation with Taz as we supervised the car loading. He was an interesting guy. Two weeks later, my wife and I received a Harry & David gift box, courtesy of my new Houston friends!

WHAT IS MOBILE?

I'm usually not at a loss for words. I picked up a rider from Seattle one afternoon at the Mobile Airport. We engaged in a little small talk.

"You know," I said, "Seattle and Mobile are in a yearly competition, and neither wants to win!"

"What do you mean?" he replied.

"We are infamous for total rainfall. One is usually #1, and the other is close behind."

Then he asked me this question, "What is Mobile?" This was not the same question as, "What is Mobile known for?" This was a 'character' question, one I had to think about.

He nodded after some 'Chamber of Commerce' talk about Mardi Gras, our seaport, the nearby beaches, and other descriptive attempts. It seemed he understood and maybe even had a little insight about my hometown. My standard retorts to those folks who say they thought Mardi Gras started in New Orleans satisfied most inquiries.

"The argument is over! Even folks from New Orleans admit that Mobile founded Mardi Gras, but they proudly declare that they 'perfected' it!" I continued. "They might have perfected it, but you have about a ninety percent better chance of getting home alive from Mobile's version!"

That usually got a chuckle.

Later, though, I thought more about that question. "What is Mobile?"

We're a city too small to be big and too big to be small. I still remember the National Geographic issue, with Mobile on the cover and a declaration that Mobile will be bigger than Atlanta, Houston, and some other southeastern cities. That never happened. That was around the same period that saw Brookley Air Force Base close, and many jobs moved out of our community.

* * *

Maybe the best way to answer "What is Mobile?" is to listen to those folks I've enjoyed driving around our town.

For example, I picked up a lady at Mobile Infirmary, about 53 years old, who was visiting her mom. The daughter was from New York, and so was her husband. Her mom had been in a horrific auto accident and had been hospitalized for months. The daughter was extremely grateful that her mom was in Mobile.

"We've never been around friendlier people in our life, and my husband has been all over the world in his airline career!"

* * *

One of the more unusual experiences with Mobile's neighborly attitude occurred when I was 'pinged' to pick up a couple at the local Lowe's store. Their accent immediately let me know that they weren't from around here. They were from South Africa and had been cruising on their large sailboat for over two years. They started from South Africa and had been all over South America, the Caribbean, the lower east coast of the United States, and the Gulf of Mexico.

Their next leg was to begin in Mobile Bay and travel north to the Great Lakes, then to New York City along a path known as the 'Great Loop.'

Without prompting, they said, "Alabama has the nicest people we have ever met!" (Note: Since Mobile is the only part of Alabama they had encountered, on behalf of our community, I accept Mobile as the cause of those high praises. No offense intended to those north of the Port City!) They were amazed that even the Coast Guard accommodated their needs when they couldn't fit into the marinas on their original plan.

Our Coast Guard escorted them to the foot of Government Street and brought them the necessary documents to facilitate their stay here in Mobile. Front-Door, First-Class Service. I'm sure they would have spread the word everywhere they traveled.

It's not just Mobile; it's our whole area and how we are raised. It's our manners. It's our nature! Just south of our city is Dauphin Island. It is not the fanciest beach in the world, but one of the friendliest—untouched by the commercialism of the resorts to our east.

* * *

Late one evening, I picked up a mother and daughter at the Mobile Airport. They were loaded with 8-10 bags of luggage and a large Weimaraner dog. They were headed for Dauphin Island. One lady was in her seventies, her daughter in her forties. The mother was a widow, and her daughter was married. They each owned beautiful homes on the island.

Their flight had been highly stressful as they had been through a three-hour argument with the authorities in their home state of Oklahoma regarding her 'therapy' dog. The daughter had a doctor's order for the dog to travel with her, not in the hold, as the airlines argued. The authorities finally relented and let the dog fly with her at her feet. Shoot, I got along great with their dog. As soon as she got in the back seat, she gave me a gigantic lick on my right ear!

I asked them why they purchased homes on Dauphin Island.

"It was truly by accident that we even learned about the place. A friend of a friend invited us, and we fell in love with the laid-back alternative to the tourist resorts, which are so well-known. We've never been around nicer people and feel so lucky to be here!"

* * *

I once picked up a lady from Ukraine whose husband was a barge captain. They'd lived all along the Gulf Coast since moving here from Ukraine. She had teenagers and said this was the friendliest place she'd lived.

What is Mobile? This is a place of history with an eye to the future. Mobile is generous. Alabama ranks as one of the most charitable states in America. Mobile is one of the leaders of this state. My daytime job is as a development director for the Little Sisters of the Poor. We receive donations from all over the United States because of the care of the Little Sisters for the elderly in our community, which began here in 1901.

We're famous for Mardi Gras and all of the parades and balls, but the number of times I give rides to people going to and from charitable events is just as remarkable. There is nothing wrong with disguising those times as fun; we do that very well.

* * *

One Saturday afternoon, I picked up a guy dressed up as The Incredible Hulk and a woman posing as Tonya Harding. They went to a '90s' theme bar crawl to raise money for a children's charity.

We have a cruise ship that attracts folks from all over the country to visit Mexico and some Caribbean ports of call. One common theme is that they wish they had more time in Mobile. "The people are so nice!"

What is Mobile? Well, we have our faults. After all, we are human. But I think Mobile is a city of manners, hope, faith in God, and a city that wants company to feel welcome.

You all should come see us! We mean it!

"I JUST NOTICED!"

I notice things like Andy Andrews talks about in his book, *The Noticer*. It's human to notice—people, appearance, attitude, mood, age, race, gender. All of those things. Those things are all surface-level. What I care about is what is just below the surface and further. Ultimately, that's the point of Andy's book. Notice the things that are not so obvious. That's what truly matters.

I've picked up folks more than 4,100 times as a ride-share driver. On average, that's at least two people per ride—more than 8,000 humans. Sometimes, I get to learn more about them than the obvious. We all have family, neighbors, folks at work, and everyday people we don't often get to know, but it's worth the effort.

I was 'dinged' to pick up a lady at a Pizza Hut. I 'saw' that she was overweight, almost toothless, and somewhat disheveled. As we talked, she seemed to be in her early thirties. She had not aged very well and appeared much older. She began our conversation by telling me that her mom was very quiet about her early childhood. Her mom was not on very good terms with her brothers and sisters, who lived up North. They had been trying to rekindle a relationship with the mom, but she refused to cooperate.

My rider said, "When I was fourteen, I was rummaging through some things in my mother's bedroom when I came upon my birth certificate. I saw my birth dad's name. About three or four years ago, I decided to try to find him."

She continued, "We met, and he told me that his wife had recently died, and he would like to see if he could reunite with my mother. My mother is married, but that didn't bother him. I'm so confused about this situation and do not know where to go with it."

When I picked her up, I saw an overweight woman with an

entire pizza in her lap, which she intended to eat all by herself. What I 'noticed' was a lonely young lady in pain who had been neglected and tossed aside all of her life. I saw someone desperately needing friendship and family, real family, to help her have joy and a sense of belonging. I hoped that her aunts and uncles would develop a positive relationship with her, even if her mother didn't seem to desire that. (I realize that I don't have any idea of the pain her mother may have experienced, so that may not be the proper remedy.)

At the Little Sisters of the Poor Sacred Heart Residence, we have more than 80 residents, four of whom have been on this earth for over 100 years. I work with nuns who have dedicated their lives to serving the elderly poor. I 'see' that they wear white habits. That's the obvious. I 'notice' the strength it takes for these amazing women to live their vows of poverty, chastity, obedience, and hospitality.

If you come to the Sacred Heart Residence, you will 'see' elderly folks traveling down the hallways, most with wheelchairs or walkers. You may also 'see' some of the Sisters or employees who care for them. You will probably 'see' volunteers or family members who visit the elderly. There is so much more to 'notice,' however.

Some residents get out of bed every morning with the desire to take care of other residents. Many residents cater to our volunteers so that their visits will be rewarding. Some volunteers take their valuable time to help people they don't know. Some employees forget that this job is paid and develop close friendships with those they serve. Some Sisters understand that the folks they pay to help them care for these elderly have lives outside of the home. Like most families, there are conflicts, but there is a shared mission—to serve!

When I first started working at the Little Sisters of the Poor, I heard a loud noise across the hall. I walked over to see what was going on. A young lady was standing with a microphone, singing to the top of her voice. A group of 'challenged' young people were putting on a show for our elderly. Only, when it was over, you couldn't tell if the young visitors were ministering to the elderly or our residents were ministering to the visitors. I 'noticed' that it didn't matter to either...they were both benefiting!

Every day in my office, I have the pleasure of a visit from one of our residents. I'm pretty sure I'm the one who gets the benefit. I've never seen her not smiling. If you were to see her, you might just 'see' an elderly lady with a cane. What I've noticed is that she's had an amazing life. Her memories of her parents, upbringing, husband, challenges, and victories are a blessing to hear. It may take a few minutes from my work, but she inspires me and reminds me of my purpose here.

The things I've 'noticed' here at Sacred Heart and in many of my Uber rides are the things that give meaning to life. I've especially noticed these things with my family and my friends. Dig below the surface, and you will notice so many other aspects of the people around you that you can't help but be fascinated with our time here.

When we discover more about the individual, rather than their outward 'identity,' we can begin solving some of the craziness in our world today. You will notice how grateful we can be for our blessings...right there, below the obvious!

"KNOW WHAT I MEAN?"

It was late on a Friday night. Friday nights are almost always the most interesting. I got a 'ding' to pick up someone near Irvington, AL. There's a raceway in Irvington, but I'm not sure what else is there.

It was a long ride to get there, and a lot of drivers would have turned it down. I pulled into the driveway, unsure if I was at the correct address.

I called him. "This is your Uber driver." I just wanted to be sure that I was in the right driveway. This was not the place to pull into the wrong driveway.

He answered, "OK, let me put my shoes on, then I'll be right out."

I was grateful he would be appropriately shod as he traveled with me. He approached the car with two beers in one hand and a phone in the other. He sat in the back right-hand seat and continued his phone conversation. He tried convincing his listener that someone had hacked his Facebook account. It checked out clean when the army discharged him. Someone was lying about him. He swore. After a few more phone calls, he apologized for the distractions.

After the phone call ended, he said the words I'm sure ride-share drivers, bartenders, and many other casual acquaintances have heard: "I probably shouldn't be saying all of this..."

I believed he had developed a relationship with me. I could tell because he kept asking me, "You know what I mean?"

I, of course, answered, "Yes, I know what you mean."

He continued, "I was lazy most of my life. I have always wanted to have my own business. That's the only way to become rich and successful. You can't get there by working to make someone else rich. Know what I mean? The problem was that I had no discipline. I would stay in bed until 2:00 pm every day. That's a lack of discipline."

I nodded in agreement.

"There is only one way I could think of to get discipline, so I joined the army. They won't let you sleep until 2:00 pm. It was the best thing I've ever done, and it's made a huge difference in my outlook on life!"

He told me that we were going to his sister's trailer. He had asked her for a favor, but she wouldn't help him in this time of need. He said he doesn't have many friends, and the few he does have only want to drink and get high.

I asked, "So, what's the favor?"

"I left my vape stuff at her trailer, and I needed it tonight. I was hoping you could take me back home when I get it from her. I even offered her $50 if she would bring it to me, but she wouldn't."

I waited outside of the trailer as he ran in. A few moments later, he ran back and jumped into the back seat.

This round trip was going to cost him at least $40.00. He continued telling me that he wanted to start a business, find the right woman to marry, and raise a lot of kids. It was his dream! He asked me what I thought and what direction he should take to get there. The woman has to be a churchgoer, which has been difficult for him to find.

"Those are wonderful dreams, but let's start at step one," I said. "What kind of business do you want to start?"

"Probably real estate," he said. "I'm thinking about buying some land and a trailer or two. I can rent those out, use the profits to expand, and eventually own a trailer park with dozens of trailers! You know what I mean?"

"Or..." he continued, "I'd like to buy or build a bar. I think there is a lot of money in bars!"

"Do you know anyone in that business? Have you ever

worked in a bar?" I asked.

"I know an old guy who used to own a bar. He and I talked about it. No matter what happens in the world, even if the economy crashes, people need a place to drink and chill out. It's foolproof! I've just got to find the right location. I think it should be in this area."

We arrived back at his house. He thanked me for the ride. I wished him good luck.

"Thanks for listening to me. Most people don't. Know what I mean?"

Yes. Yes, I do.

"REDNECKS WITH PAYCHECKS!"

This is one of my weirdest titles, but the story is amazing. Friday night, November 1st, Uber pinged me to go to the Mobile Airport. There is a 'ride-share' parking lot where most Uber and Lyft rides originate, so getting a request away from the airport is sometimes unusual. It turned out the whole ride was unusual.

I picked up a very friendly young man. The app showed that we were going to Leakesville, MS. According to the app, we were about an hour away from the destination. Some riders are quiet, but I try to engage them in a friendly manner. It usually makes the trip go quicker.

I could tell right away this was going to be a quick trip. Derrick was very personable and engaging. He flew into Mobile from Dallas. We had a great conversation. He told me about his life. I told him about mine. I wish the trip had lasted longer! (Truthfully, it lasted longer than expected once I dropped him off. I'll talk more about that later.)

"What's going on in Leakesville? I don't think I've ever been there," I asked.

"I'm going to compete in a big 'Off-Road' race with a truck I've never driven. It's a little intimidating. I'm excited about it, though!" said Derrick.

I wondered how he got into this world. I loved his story!

"My family grew up in St. Joe, Texas. My great-grandfather bought his ranch in 1904. He sold it when I was a young child. The property came up for sale while my grandparents were still alive, in their 90s, and I wanted to make them proud by buying it.

"I scraped up enough money to make the down payment, even though I didn't qualify for traditional financing. I had no idea how I was going to make the payments. That was so stressful.

"I remember trying to figure out what I could do with the property. As I stood there looking at it, the idea of an off-road racing facility came to my mind. I don't know why. I had never even seen an off-road race.

"I had a friend who was a successful businessman. In his 'off-time' he wore overalls and spit snuff, often dribbling down his chin. He had a tractor and helped me grade the property to be race-suitable. Our first couple of race events were small and painfully unsuccessful.

"Someone with a lot of experience told me my problem was that I had targeted folks with very little money. He told me that I seemed to be going after a bunch of hillbillies. That's when I started thinking differently, which is where my business name came from."

He continued, "Hillbillies and rednecks! I need folks with real dollars. It came to me—*Rednecks With Paychecks!* That was my target. It has worked out very well. We hold two main events each year."

Derrick then said, "You remember the hurricane that hit Houston a couple of years ago? I was out on my property preparing for an upcoming event when I got a call from a friend. He asked me if I'd heard what was going on in Houston. There was massive flooding, and lots of people were in trouble. They needed help, he told me.

"I've got an event in three weeks, I told him. He didn't back down. I got on the phone and contacted as many guys as possible who had access to these monster trucks. We formed a huge caravan to help. The opposite happened even though they said the rescue folks there would probably turn us around. Our vehicles could go to so many places that the rescue vehicles couldn't. Even the boats had problems with their propellers tearing up on submerged cars they couldn't see.

"We were there for about a week, along with the 'Cajun Navy' from Louisiana. At that point, President Trump and his wife, Melania, came to thank the folks who helped. Somehow, I was told I was one of about thirty and could bring one person with me to a special function to meet the president and his wife.

"I was amazed at how grateful and friendly President Trump was to us. He was genuinely interested and made you feel like you were the only person he cared to hear from. No looking around to see who might be more important. A little later, Mrs. Trump approached me and complimented me on my cowboy hat. She sat by me for a long time, making me feel like we were good friends. I had no idea how beautiful she was in person, and I am still amazed by how she never acted like she was above all of us.

"After all of this, a BBC reporter from Great Britain asked if he could spend some time at my upcoming event. He said he wanted to learn more about us. I invited him to stay at my house. I began to worry about his motives when it seemed he asked the same questions of everyone he met."

The reporter had asked him, "Why do you people support Trump? Why are there so many rebel flags everywhere? What is the 'redneck' culture all about?"

The reporter spent several days with Derrick and the folks in St. Joe. Derrick told me that they involved him in every aspect of the community, including barbecues and the hard work as they prepared for the off-road event. People from all walks of life attend these functions. Combined with the efforts in Houston, it was evident that someone's race, creed, or color was of no consequence to those in the rescue effort. At the end of his time with them, the reporter broke down as they said their goodbyes.

"I had no idea what kind of people all of you really are in Texas," he said. "I've heard of southern hospitality, but I had no idea what that meant. The outside world has a totally untrue vision of the people here. I hope to do my small part to change that perception."

Derrick told me his story would be aired in a BBC special soon. He also showed me a video about the Houston story.

Derrick was a true American success story. I enjoyed this ride. When we arrived at the venue, he continued to be cordial as he showed me around. There were off-road vehicles of all types and sizes moving all around us. One of these days, I'd like to attend an event.

There's one more lesson I learned after dropping him off in Leakesville. We have become entirely too dependent on technology. AT&T gave us no signal for the last 5-10 miles to our destination, which meant no maps. On our way there, I'm sure we had taken some back roads to reduce the mileage and time. Twice during these diversions, we shared the road with deer, one of which ran right in front of my car. A third deer incident happened as I made my way home.

Because there was no reception, my Uber app would not let me show that I had dropped Derrick off. In the darkness, I also missed a turn or two and had only the compass on my rear-view mirror as a navigation tool. I naturally headed east on a four-lane highway, thinking that was the direction back to Mobile. That eventually turned northeast, then due north. Uh-oh.

I made a U-turn and headed back in the other direction. Once I was south of Leakesville, my reception improved enough to see a question from the Uber app. *'Did you drop off your rider?'*

I hit 'yes' and immediately began dialing the Uber helpline. From the amount Uber charged Derrick, I knew he had probably overpaid. After about 25 minutes on hold and 15 minutes of explaining to a voice from another part of the planet, I got it corrected.

Just another average night as an Uber driver!

Thanks again, Derrick!

"LISTENING TO LIFE'S LESSONS!"

It had been three years! In a few weeks, I was about to complete my three years of driving for Uber. I was grateful for something I never anticipated when I began this venture. I still had a long way to go, but I was slowly learning to listen. More than 9,000 riders had been passengers in my Hyundai Santa Fe then.

I still laugh when I think back to a comedian who asked, "What is it about Uber drivers that makes them want to carry on a conversation on every ride? I never had that when we used to take taxis!"

I don't understand why people open up in these instances, but they do. I had picked up a young lady from Ukraine several months ago. She opened up about her family back home and how different life was for them.

She told me, "I call home a few times each week to see how they're doing. Their answer to me was that they were all fine."

She continued, "My dad had some health issues, but they continued to tell me that he was doing okay. That was their answer until one of my recent calls. They informed me that Dad had just been released from the hospital and had lost a lung to cancer!"

She was distraught that the medical profession over there was so inept. They had not detected cancer in any previous examination, even though they now claimed he suffered from cancer for quite a long time.

"This has had a terrible effect on our family. I haven't been home for over three years, but I'm planning a surprise visit in a few weeks. Had I known the truth about my father's health, I would have spent more time with him."

Sometimes, the 'reward' comes from eavesdropping. I know that sounds rude, but most riders do not attempt discretion. This young lady worked for an engineering firm in Montgomery. She was in town for a conference and asked for my indulgence while she made a call to her father. She told me that she usually called him on trips like this. He was retired from the same industry.

I found her conversation touching as she talked to him about getting together for lunch when she returned home. He was giving advice of some sort, which she appreciated. She told him at least four times that she loved him.

When she hung up, she said to me, "Someday, he won't be around anymore. I try to make every contact with my dad a special one!"

* * *

One more story:

Some Saturday mornings, I pick up folks leaving Mobile on the Carnival cruise ship *Fantasy*. These are almost always positive experiences! These folks are excited about their vacation and always in a good mood.

Uber summoned me to pick up a couple from their hotel just on the other side of the causeway. This is usually a 15-minute ride. Not today. The cruise ship was very late getting to port because of heavy fog. This caused delays for the departing guests and the cleaning and prepping crews, which delayed the arriving passengers.

My 15-minute trip turned into a 105-minute ride. I don't know who apologized more. Me, for the vacation delay, or my riders for tying me up on one fare for that long. Neither of us was to blame, so we decided to make the best of the situation.

The husband, in his late thirties, told me that he owned his own business. He said, "I used to work in a family business, but that turned into a disaster." Now, he had ventured into my field of expertise.

We shared stories of challenges, both personal and business experiences. When his father passed away, they had no clear plan of succession, nor did they have a good feel for the responsibilities to be handled by him and his brother.

To make matters worse, the business suffered a considerable downturn, which caused his brother to leave and eventually led to the company's demise. Their split had been very caustic and divisive. Sometime after that, he started his own company in the same field.

He got a phone call. "We're a little delayed, but we've got a nice driver, and we're just relaxing, waiting for our turn to board the ship!"

Of course, I was pleased he seemed so relaxed. It could have been much worse.

He continued a light-hearted discussion. Then came the surprise! Just before he hung up, he said, "Can't wait to see y'all when we get back! Y'all take care. I love you!"

He hung up and said, "That was my brother. He's started working with me again. This time, we clearly have a separation of duties, and I'm the 100% owner. He's more of a technician and is so much happier staying out of the business end of everything."

When we finally reached the ship, he and his wife gathered their luggage, and each hugged me. In less than two hours, we became friends. We won't see each other again, but I won't forget the lesson. I bet their cruise was fantastic. He would never believe less! I love that attitude!

"THUMBS UP!"

Life boils down to attitude and your chosen view of everything around you. If perception is reality, then reality can be changed by our perception, something I believe we can significantly affect.

That day, I picked up a young lady from just north of Mobile. As always, I asked her how her day was going. Usually, my rider will answer, "Pretty good!" or something along that line. Not this time.

"I can't wait to get out of here," she said. "This is the worst place I've ever lived when it comes to public transportation! If you don't have a car, you are nobody! I've got two kids in terrible schools here, and we're not close enough to grocery stores. When my children leave school, there is nothing for them to do. They have some after-school care, but they should do more for them."

I asked her, "So, where are you from?"

"I'm from Kansas City, Missouri. It's about two hours from St. Louis."

(I think she anticipated my response, but I couldn't bring myself to ask it nicely.)

She continued, "The crime rate is terrible there. My kids won't have a chance, but as soon as it gets better, I'm going back! At least there they have discounts for buses and other public transportation. Here, unless you live in a wealthy neighborhood, no one gives a !@$#% about you!"

At this point, I just nodded and said, "Well, I hope everything gets better!" There's not much else one could say. I was just hoping to avoid a low rating at this point.

* * *

Here's another view. I picked up a young man with a level of energy that was simply contagious. He didn't have his vehicle then, but you could tell he was on fire.

"How's your day going?" I asked.

"It's one of the best days of my life! I sell home security systems door-to-door, and this has been one of my team's best weeks!"

As I said, it becomes contagious. "Tell me what's going on!" I continued.

"I've been doing this for five years now. I've worked my way up to supervisor over twelve other salespeople. I'm twenty-two years old. It isn't always easy. Mobile and New Orleans are the toughest areas to get going. People here are not as open to folks knocking at their door, but we just keep trying."

"Maybe it has to do with some bad experiences in the past after hurricanes," I explained. "A lot of shyster sales folks trying to make a quick buck."

"I understand that, but we're making progress! This has been one of my best weeks. I don't do as much selling anymore. I'm the one who follows up after my team and makes sure that we get everything done that we've promised. A lot of our business now comes from referrals."

Somewhere in the conversation, he told me that someone wrecked into his car, so he didn't have transportation right now. He used Uber and Lyft to get the job done.

I'm not saying that his 'attitude' would change public transportation, nor am I insisting that his perception will improve the school system. Maybe I should take that back. There is an excellent chance that someone with his attitude can make a difference.

Chresal Threadgill, superintendent of the Mobile County Public Schools, spoke to our Rotary Club a few weeks after this encounter. I'm pleased to say he had an attitude closer to the one in my second example. I have high hopes that he will make a positive difference.

"CELEBRATE! IT'S FRIDAY!"

"We're here!" I told my rider.

He was asleep.

"Excuse me, sir... We've arrived at your hotel."

He still seemed confused.

This gentleman was standing alone on a corner in downtown Mobile twenty minutes earlier. He was an older African-American man outside of a cigar bar. At 1:38 am, I arrived. I asked his name to make sure he was my rider.

He said at least three times while entering the car, "Thank you. Thank you. Thank you."

I smelled the aroma of his cigar, still in his hand. "I'm sorry, sir. You can't smoke that in my car." I glanced to the back passenger-side seat and saw that the partially smoked cigar was not lit.

He said, "Oh, I'm gonna finish it later; I just didn't want to throw it away. I'm here to celebrate my daughter's graduation in nursing at the University of South Alabama! We're so proud of her! I'm from Chicago. Most of our family is in the South. I guess I'm the only one left up North," he told me. "Thank you!"

I could tell he was tired. His only response continued to be, "Thank you for picking me up...thank you..."

We finally reached his hotel. It was close to 2:00 am, and I'd already accepted another ride. "Sir, we're here. Time to go."

He looked to his right at the entrance door to the hotel. "This is not where I'm supposed to be."

"Well, this is what you put in the app. Where are you supposed to be?" I asked.

"I'm supposed to be at 322 South State Street. That's where

I live."

"That must be your Chicago home. You're in Mobile, Alabama, for your granddaughter's graduation."

He stared at me, then at the front door. He tried to get his bearings. Finally, he thanked me several more times and turned down my offer to help him to the entrance.

His was one of 27 rides I gave on this night. It had been a long night but a productive day. The holiday season meant office parties, family gatherings, and Mardi Gras Societies in Mobile. This night brought the annual 'Santa Claus Society' event. Most of my rides began with picking up these young men dressed in their Santa attire and delivering them to a downtown venue for the pre-party party. Many of these gentlemen had obviously attended a 'pre-pre-party.'

* * *

The next series of rides belonged mainly to the young ladies who the aforementioned Kris Kringle impersonators would escort. Again, several of these lovely young ladies, clad in their finest evening gowns, had also begun their festivities before the main event.

Now, it was time for the new veterans. These brave souls had graduated to the next level of seniority and combined a mix of nostalgia with gratitude that their days of revelry had tempered. They exuded just the proper enthusiasm and a firm grasp of recovery time. They had often adjusted their schedules to meet the next generation of revelers' demands: babies and small children. They woke up at their regular time regardless of their parent's schedule. Or they would wake up at a grandparents' home.

Finally, we experienced the generation of party-goers who realized they'd like to be 'involved' in the activities at a level that precluded driving personally to and from the venue. This generation fit snugly in the middle of the evening. They were the last to go and the first to return. They were most likely described as 'genteel.'

The night progressed quickly. The rides came one after another. I picked up strangers, friends, acquaintances, folks excited about the evening ahead of them, and folks ready to call it a day. Among all of these party-goers, some folks were just grateful that someone was there to get them home. Or, at least, to their hotel where they could get some rest, wake up, and attend a granddaughter's graduation from nursing school.

Riders often ask me if I enjoy Ubering. My honest answer is, "I do!"

But what I enjoy the most is studying human behavior. Even while my riders are partying, I'm fascinated by the interaction and especially the roles played by my riders with each other. In a few weeks, I'll reach my 5,000th ride. Education is priceless! I'm still learning.

"FRIENDS?"

I had given her a ride twice before. She had a charming demeanor as she shared stories about her work. Not so much about the mechanics of her security guard job but about the shift times. I picked Jalisa up just after 8:15 pm as she completed her work day. She fancied herself a 'night' person.

Jalisa lived in Saraland, which gave us about 15-20 minutes together. I could tell she was a little tired, more than usual.

"How's your day been?" I asked.

Jalisa paused for a moment. "I've lived in the same house for over fourteen years. I've raised my four kids there. Only one of them is still living with me.

"He's in high school for three more years and will probably join his two brothers in the military when he graduates. My daughter is in college, and I don't believe she'll return to this area when she graduates in three or four years.

"I have had the opportunity to buy my home several times, but when my landlord offered to sell it to me, she backed out each time. So I've put a lot of my own time and money into that home."

"What will you do when your son is gone, and it's just you?" I asked.

"I still want to buy this home. I love it here. I'm 47 years old, and I want to own my place. I've thought about moving close to my daughter but would still be renting. It wouldn't make sense to buy in a place where I wouldn't know anyone after my daughter left," Jalisa said. "Besides, I love living here. I'm used to my surroundings."

I sensed a feeling of surrender in her voice.

"If you stayed here, you would still be around your friends. Maybe you could travel to visit kids and grandkids wherever they are?" I said.

That's when she surprised me with her answer. Jalisa struck me as so personable and friendly.

"I don't have any real friends. I get up every morning, go through my daily routine, go to work, and return. I'm around other people; I just don't really think of them as friends."

I had no idea where the father of her children was in the scheme of things. She still maintained some level of communication with her kids, but it seemed like it needed to be more consistent, based on her remarks.

Our ride was ending. I hoped Jalisa was having an unusually tough day and that she was exaggerating the lack of friendship.

"The good news," I told her, "is that you still have time to think about what you want to do long-term. I'm sure you have friends you haven't even noticed yet. I'll be praying for you!"

"Thanks," said Jalisa. "I hope so."

Sometimes, my rides are for my benefit. Jalisa was one of those.

She reminded me of how lucky I am. I'm so grateful for family and friends who helped me cherish my days. I can't even imagine life without them.

I hope Jalisa finds some friends and opens her heart to them. There are too many people like her who deserve the blessing.

"YOUTHFUL EXUBERANCE!"

I love the unbridled confidence and enthusiasm of some of my younger riders.

I picked up Jeffrey, 18, who was about to graduate from high school the following week. I was taking him to a restaurant in Baldwin County, where he had just started a new job. He would be using the income from that job to move to an apartment with a buddy. He was ready to be self-sufficient and would not be attending college.

I asked him if he wanted to have a career in the restaurant business.

He replied, "No, but I have to start somewhere! I want to be a writer!"

I told him I was a writer and had published a book. He became excited and asked if I liked reading horror/science fiction books. He named off at least a dozen titles I'd yet to hear of. It didn't matter. Jeffrey gave me the gory details of futuristic horror themes from at least 250 titles for the next ten minutes.

When we reached his destination, he thanked me for the ride. He also said, "I appreciate your encouragement! You make me believe I can do this!"

(Those who know me won't believe this, but I don't think I said more than ten words during our ride. It also should have occurred to him that his 'mentor' was driving an Uber instead of relaxing on a beach somewhere, living off the massive royalties from my many best-sellers.)

* * *

I've also picked up young folks actively working toward their dreams. Marvin is an example. He was a musician who was working his way through college. He often brought his guitar with him as he went to his part-time job working at a tennis club office. He practiced on one of his many guitars when it was not busy.

He played at local events, sometimes solo and sometimes with other musicians. I mentioned to him that I once took guitar lessons as a youth. (After my first recital, my teacher and I decided I should try something less destructive.) Marvin took my failure as a challenge and described the best type of guitar to learn, brought one for me to look at on one of our rides, and offered to teach me as soon as I was ready.

He taught guitar lessons on the side now. I didn't have the heart to tell him that my friends and family had banned me from anything that made noise in the pursuit of music on my part. You had to love his enthusiasm. I am more confident in him than the part-time restauranteur/horror author I mentioned earlier.

Sometimes, I talked to a young non-rider who genuinely desired to learn and achieve. I get my car washed every day that I drive.

Once, halfway through the car wash, the mechanism jammed, and I was trapped. I already had a pickup on the app.

I told the young attendant how much I would lose if he didn't get this thing moving immediately. He apologized and assured me that the other attendant had fixed this problem often and we shouldn't have to wait much longer.

"How do you track what you make by Ubering?" he asked. "I want to go into business someday, and I'm always curious how people keep up."

I paused momentarily as we both heard my app exclaim, "Rider has canceled!"

I turned the app off until they could free me. I had a captive audience of approximately one 18-year-old. We started talking about spreadsheets and percentages.

"I want to write comic books and learn to be an illustrator online. I have already done some good work. Do you have a card or something if I want to ask you some questions about those spreadsheets?" he said.

I gave him my card. I liked his attitude and his confidence. I didn't know if he'd ever call, but he did a great job of making the time pass for me. He might need to remember why he had a card from a guy at a nursing home. I'd love to hear from him.

I've got so many other stories. One thing they all have in common is hope.

"STORY TIME!"

I love stories! One of the advantages I've enjoyed while driving for Uber is the opportunity to tell stories my family and friends are tired of hearing. I get new audiences all the time. But everybody has a story to tell, and I enjoy listening to theirs.

I spent many years speaking around the country, especially when I was involved in the Jaycees. One of the organizations that helped me hone my stories was the Toastmasters. Many years ago, one of our members asked me to mentor him while he was a new member of Toastmasters.

He said, "I don't have any stories. You and the other members have stories in your lives, which makes it easier to be an interesting speaker."

"Everyone has stories," I told him. "It's part of being human. You need to pay attention to the things happening around you."

We briefly discussed his family, jobs, education, and other life experiences. He mentioned he was a conductor on the Amtrak Sunset Limited train in 1993.

"You might remember the train wreck on Bayou Canot," he said. "It was the most deadly Amtrak train wreck in history."

A fog-stricken barge had collided with the bridge on that fateful morning. The train left New Orleans that morning but received no warning because the barge had displaced parts of the bridge, which was not enough damage to cause an alert. The tragic accident killed forty-seven people and injured more than 100 others.

He continued, "I was supposed to be a conductor on that train that day. I was sick and called for a replacement. He was also a good friend of mine. He died that morning."

We went on to talk about other, much more benign stories of his life. This came from a man who said he didn't have stories like the rest of us. He was right. He was unsure if he wanted to recall the conductor's story repeatedly.

I understand that feeling. But, as exciting and tragic as his story was, his response and the lessons he learned were more important and valuable to listeners.

I've had more than 8,000 rides since I began Ubering. Most of them were too short for significant conversation, but the stories I did hear—wow!

* * *

I picked up a guy named Nicholas, who had gone viral on YouTube for being in a helicopter crash on I-10 in Louisiana. He wasn't in the helicopter. He was driving an 18-wheeler when the aircraft crashed right in front of him. His truck ran into the flaming wreckage, which continued breaking apart in the road ahead.

His blow-by-blow description of what he had experienced was captivating.

That's a story he would never forget.

* * *

Another rider of note: Mac Daddy Duds! I picked him up at Langan (Municipal) Park in Mobile. I wasn't up on my Diamond Professional Wrestling stars, so I didn't recognize my passenger. He was a former champion. I looked him up online later. What a personality!

He told me he dove the lakes at Langan Park to retrieve frisbees for his Disc Golf business. The name was Dud's Disc Diving/Gamers & Geeks. His stories were interesting, but there was one discussion I found most intriguing.

He had discovered two pistols in the Langan Park lakes. He turned them both over to the Mobile Police Department, with one traceable to an active crime investigation suspect. Mac Daddy Dud could tell a story!

Yep! One of the aspects of ride-sharing that keeps me going is the opportunity to share stories. People are the most intriguing animals on this planet. Take some time to listen to their stories!

"DAY DANCING!"

It had been several months since I'd picked up Jeremy. Each time I gave him a ride, it was late morning or early afternoon. Most rides began at one 'pub' and ended at another. Sometimes, I gave him a ride to his parent's house.

Jeremy appeared to be in his late forties or early fifties. He was in Satsuma to take care of his parents. His mother had cancer, and his father suffered from a malady Jeremy failed to disclose.

I remember the first time I gave a ride to Jeremy. It was about 11:00 am. He limped out of the bar and sat in the front passenger seat.

"It takes me a little longer to get places with this fake leg," he said. "I'm back from New Zealand to care for my parents."

"So, what do you do in New Zealand?" I asked.

After several minutes of discussion, the best I could guess was that he was involved in some technical security services. Jeremy wasn't just a technician, though. He claimed to be on the cutting edge of innovation and told me about his high-security clearances.

He described the various foreign countries in which his vocation took him. Frankly, I was fascinated by his stories, even if I couldn't be sure of their authenticity.

We pulled up to his destination—another bar. "Sylvia has the best breakfast in the county! I've known her for years. She has a very loyal following here." (The only evidence I could see was a pickup truck next to the front door. But it was just 11:30 am.)

We would repeat this cycle several times. Each time, he would say, "You remember me, right?" Then, he would continue his stories as though he recalled precisely where we left off. Sometimes I dropped him off at his parent's place.

Nothing in Jeremy's demeanor, nor his family's property, would lead one to think of him as a world traveler, but each trip would elicit a different adventure.

"My mom seems to be getting better, so I'll be heading back to New Zealand soon."

It was about a year before I saw him again. Things hadn't changed much when I picked him up then. Again, it was early afternoon at the same establishment where I first met him. The destination was also the same: Sylvia's Bar.

"You remember me, I'm sure!" he said.

"Of course I do!" I answered. "How have you been?"

"I came back home to take care of my parents. They're getting a little better, but they're both still in rough shape. We agree it's time for me to hit the road again, though."

"Going back to New Zealand?" I asked.

"No. I'm going to Gdansk, Poland. I'll be meeting some friends over there. We're going to a heavy metal dance party near there. I'll be in Eastern Europe for at least six months. I'll be dancing up a storm in several countries."

I hate to admit it, and maybe I'm improperly stereotyping. However, picturing a fifty-year-old, one-legged, overweight, mid-Generation 'X' day drinker floating over a mosh-pit is beyond my imagination.

"I may not be able to walk or run very well, but I can really shake this one leg! Dancing is probably my favorite pastime. You oughta see me!"

We reached his destination. As he struggled to get out of the car, he gave me the exact parting phrase he always did, "Five stars and a good tip! Thanks for the ride!"

I would love to see a video with Jeremy shaking that leg in the middle of his heavy metal favorites. Quite a show, I'm sure!

"TRI-FECTA!"

I read somewhere that humans are fascinated by things that come in threes. I know I am. We compare and contrast people and events as a trio.

So, my first rider in this story was also the youngest. He attended a local high school, and I picked him up after an on-campus football game. He told me he played on the team last year but quit to put more time into his studies.

"I flunked a few courses, but I hope to pass them this time," he explained. "I'm working harder than ever!"

I have to admit; I was concerned that he admitted to putting off core courses to pass classes that didn't sound like any I'd heard of before. At least he recognized that he had to improve his work ethic.

* * *

The next young man I picked up was ten years older than my previous subject. He had also struggled with his livelihood. He spent several years working as a mechanic but couldn't or wouldn't hold onto a steady position at more than a few garages.

"I think I've found the best way to be successful now, though!" he said. "I'm going to college, and it's really helped!" The enthusiasm in his voice was palpable.

"Where are you going to college?" I asked.

"They call it Toyota University. They train us in particular areas so that we become experts in their shops. I'm learning the a/c specialty, but I've already learned other areas. They pay me while I'm learning."

I loved the idea that he would learn several different skills and eventually specialize in something he would love with solid proof of his effectiveness. My hats off to Toyota. I know some other companies use the strategy, but I'd like to see the technique grow.

* * *

Finally, I picked up a divorced dad for a round trip with two stops before the return home. He had moved to Mobile from California and a few other Western states to be with his mom and dad. They were both in bad health and eventually passed away.

He admitted to spending most of his life out West as 'a knucklehead!' Drugs and crime played a role in his lifestyle. During that time, he fathered four children, two of whom were grown and out in the world. His fifteen-year-old son had come to Mobile to live with him. The kid's mother could no longer handle the boy.

"He's my knucklehead! Doesn't listen to anything his mom tells him, and she's fed up. I'm trying to get him in line. I've put him in a new school. He's lived a little in Mobile before, so he still has some friends here."

My rider's phone rang.

"Hi, son," he answered. "What up? I've left the house for a few errands. It's all locked up tight. You can't get in!" The son didn't have a key.

We stopped first at a Family Dollar store. He returned quickly. We were on to our second stop, the liquor store. We talked about the challenges of raising a teenager in these times. That period has always been challenging!

We saw four guys walking down the middle of the street as we approached his home.

"See that tall one in the middle with the hoodie? That's my boy. I've got most of my knucklehead life straightened out, but it looks like he and I have a lot of work to do together."

I felt he still had a little learning to do himself. You never know; maybe the responsibility will help both grow up better. I hope so!

Three rides. Three different views of life. Three ways of growing up.

"LISTEN TO THE LIGHTHOUSE!"

I tend to think in threes. It could be finding a problem, seeing the challenge in practice, and contemplating a solution. Some of my riders that week caused me to notice a pattern. Here's what I mean.

I got a ding to pick up a gentleman near Brookley Field. He hopped in the back seat and immediately told me, "We've got about 22 minutes until I get home. I love to carry on conversations with my Uber drivers, so tell me something about yourself!"

Anyone who knows me knows that I hate talking about myself! And anyone who knows me knows that's a lie! The challenge is doing it in the mere 22 minutes we have together. But I gave it my best effort!

After about three or four minutes, I asked him, "So, tell me what you're all about. I already know everything about me!"

We had a great 'back and forth' for several minutes. Here is a quick synopsis of our agreements. There is evil in the world. Most people are good people but don't have enough positive role models. He pointed out some neighborhoods we passed through, which he was familiar with.

"Bad role models influence the young folks here. I know because I grew up around them," he said. "It took some mistakes on my part before I decided to change my life."

That was part one.

* * *

Later, I picked up a lady in her early 50s. She took up where the gentleman had left off.

"I am so worried about my grandchildren. My daughter has two kids from two men and is living with another man. Nobody knows where the other two fathers are. Half the time, my granddaughter is left to take care of her little brother alone.

She's only sixteen."

She continued, "I've begged my granddaughter to be the one who breaks the cycle. I was just as bad as my daughter at trying to have a decent family. I hope she listens to me. She sees what a mess it is for all of us."

I thought to myself, *at least the granddaughter has someone telling her the truth.* I've heard these same stories at least fifty times during my Uber driving. I get frustrated.

And then the third part.

* * *

I picked up a wonderful couple who had asked me to take them to a company function and give them a ride home afterward. I had known the husband for many years, but mainly from a distance.

Their home was quite a distance from the event. Despite what I said earlier in this chapter, I tend to talk as much as anyone will allow, especially about myself. But, on the ride home, I switched mainly to the listener mode. I'm glad I did.

I'm not at liberty to mention the gentleman's name, but I had heard about a mentoring program in the Mobile area. He was heavily involved in the effort. His wife also worked to have a positive experience in people's lives through their interaction with animals.

He mentored at least six young men through a program that provided the kind of role models that countered the culture that affected the lives of these young men.

I asked him, "Do you think you've successfully turned their lives around?"

"I believe that at least one young man has responded very well. He's started along a path that gives him a real chance of success. He could be the one that breaks the cycle we talked about earlier."

I have to admit that this couple lifted my spirits dramatically. Their real-life jobs helped people navigate challenges in their lives. Lots of people separated their careers from their personal lives. Theirs was seamless. I meet a lot of people like them, but we need more.

I see people like these folks as lighthouses. They demonstrate life's possibilities to the lost and provide the means for their pursuit of success. It shows in their actions and, more importantly, their faith in God.

My first rider above described the problem. The second was actively living and challenging the status quo but needed more tools. The third couple was providing solutions throughout their lives. The Lighthouses!

Someone asked me that day if I would quit driving after retiring from my regular career. I genuinely don't know. In almost seven years of Ubering, I've learned more about people from around this planet than anything else I've done.

I may stop driving folks once I've learned to listen more than I talk. Could be a little while yet!

"FAMILY'S DOLLAR!"

I've been ride-sharing for almost seven years now. I've driven for Uber and Lyft and delivered food for Uber Eats and DoorDash during the pandemic. I've written more than 143 blogs since I started. Thirty-seven were politically oriented, but the rest were stories of my riders or my 'slice-of-life' experiences.

I'm delighted that Lagniappe Weekly will begin including my blogs in their publication, starting with this one. I started writing the stories in January 2019 because so many people kept asking, "What's your most memorable Uber story?" or "What's the craziest thing that ever happened to you?"

Ride-sharing is a part-time gig for me. I work full-time as the development director at the Little Sisters of the Poor. So, I do most of my Ubering on nights and weekends. I've completed more than 9,000 rides with at least 17,000 passengers. My riders have come from at least sixty-five different countries.

I'm never short of stories of people from all walks of life. I'm fascinated by their lives. Sometimes, they tell me their stories on purpose, but often, I learn about them from their conversations with others or by seeing the communities in which they spend their time.

That week, I got to experience one of those special rides that shine a light on why I keep driving.

I was close to my quitting time for the night when I got one more ding to pick someone up. Uber tells us when they summon us how long it will take to reach our pickup and how long it will take for the actual ride. My final ride for the evening would take me twenty minutes further away from my home.

I arrived somewhere in the middle of Baldwin County at a Family Dollar store. There were no cars in the parking lot. I saw a woman and her son waving at me outside the store. They have several large bags, which we loaded into the back of the car.

"How's your day going?" I asked.

"This is a great day for us!" the mother responded. "My son just got paid for his new job, and we could finally afford to get some things we needed at home. It was getting real tight."

Her son appeared to be around twenty years old. He was very excited. "I work at Bucee's!" he said. "I make $21.00 per hour and $42.00 per hour on Thanksgiving Day. My old job paid $13.00 per hour. I love working at Bucee's!"

These two seemed overly excited about the trip to Family Dollar. I started to understand more as they told me their story.

"The two of us are all that's left of our family. I guess we're considered the black sheep of the family," she said. "My son has special needs and is the only one bringing any money home for us right now."

"You must be very proud of him!" I responded.

"I am very proud of him!" she said.

At the same time, he was saying, "She's proud of me, and I'm proud of me!"

I have to admit, all three of us were proud of him! We spent the next several minutes discussing his plans to work hard enough to get a car they could use. He told me that he did any job that needed to be done at Bucee's. No challenge was too big for him!

I don't believe I've ever seen two people more enthused by a shopping trip to Family Dollar. No offense to Family Dollar. They named off all the things his paycheck bought that night. Most of us take these things for granted. Heck, they purchased the gigantic 2-ply jumbo package of toilet paper!

We turned into a dirt road on the approach to their trailer park. The muddy road ended in the middle of a low-lighted group of about two or three reasonably nice homes. I offered to help them carry their bags, which they declined.

They walked past the nice trailers toward a few well-seasoned versions of mobile homes. He turned around and thanked me for the ride as they faded into the darkened woods. There was something extraordinary about that young man. He made his mom proud!

* * *

Over the years, I've picked up people from all levels of society. My passengers have been political and business leaders, people who want to be responsible, those with no other means of transportation, and out-of-towners who see us as the best way to get to their venues.

I've broken nearly every rule of polite conversation, including politics, religion, family dynamics, and so much more. Just before the 2023 SEC Championship, I picked up a couple from Georgia who had just finished a delicious late-night dinner at Felix's on the Causeway.

The husband and I had a great conversation about whether the SEC would be represented in the Final Four Playoff if Bama beat the Dawgs. The debate continued at the destination hotel. The gentleman and I conceded our best wishes to each other and our teams. Unfortunately, that was several minutes after his wife had left to go inside.

"FLASH DRIVE!"

"My life flashed before my eyes!"

We've all heard that phrase before. That thought crossed my mind on one of my recent Uber drive nights. Our population is genuinely diverse, at least when considering the ride-share driver's experiences.

I average eight rides per night when driving during the week. Most rides are routine, but I collected more than my share of 'unique' passengers that week.

One of my first rides was to pick up a gentleman at the bus station. 'Richard' had arrived from Destin and was going to spend a few weeks in Mobile. He appeared to be in his late 30s. His life was a mess. After spending time in drug rehab somewhere in Mobile, he would be making a trip to Tennessee to start a new life.

Richard credited his mom and his sister for not giving up on him. He said, "I gave up on myself a long time ago. They never did. I owe them a turnaround."

* * *

Uber 'pre-announced' my next rider. Sometimes, a passenger may have special needs. The rider may have physical disabilities, pets, or other challenges. This one was easy.

"The elderly rider may need extra care entering and exiting the vehicle," Uber said. If you're uncomfortable, Uber lets you opt out. I've never opted out. Besides, I worked in a nursing home during the day.

I arrived at the shopping center where my rider was waiting. I helped her to the car. While she needed ambulatory help, her mind was sharp. Rather than someone who was in need, she was one of the sweetest people I'd ever met. We had a wonderful conversation. What a pleasant surprise!

* * *

Two rides later, I picked up two young men and a young lady in Prichard. We were heading toward Semmes. One of the young men rode up front. We had a great conversation as we took the final turn onto their street. The road needed repair and was narrower than average, barely a two-lane road. No streetlights.

We all noticed a pickup truck ahead on the left side of the road. The truck was facing the same direction as us but was on the wrong side. The passenger side front door was open, which would leave us barely enough room to pass. There was something else unusual.

A fairly large woman was standing next to the open door facing us. As we approached her, she seemed to be half-dressed. Then our lights hit her. She appeared to be wearing a black string bikini and was trying to pull up tight jeans.

That's when it hit us. Those weren't bikini bottoms. When you are sitting in a vehicle, your eyes are at an unfortunate level. Ergo, *"FLASH"* as referred to in today's title.

"Well," I said, "that was certainly different."

My riders spoke up quickly. "Hey, we want you to know that was different for us, too! We live two doors down from here, and we want you to know that is very unusual! We're in a nice neighborhood!"

I asked, "Did any of you recognize her?"

All of us had to admit that we never saw her face. The ride ended in laughter.

The night wasn't over, though.

* * *

My last ride came from a local hospital emergency room. The rider called me immediately after she booked the ride.

"I've never used Uber before. I put my credit card in, and I need you to pick me up now! I can't walk very well, but I have to get out of here before I go crazy! My wait time to see a doctor is at least six hours, and an older lady here is moaning very loudly."

This had to be fun. I told her I'd put my flashers (not a reference to the previous story) outside the emergency entrance. She didn't come out. I called her.

"You're going to have to come in and get me. I can't walk, and I don't have any shoes on!"

She told me her story as we headed toward her parent's home. "I've been in and out of the hospital for different reasons. My brain is not communicating with my leg. My dad told me to wait and go to the doc-in-a-box tomorrow, but I was scared I was having a stroke or something. I came here in an ambulance.

"I've been through a lot in my life. I was at the Home of Grace for Women long ago." (Note: I served on their Board of Directors in the late 80s and early 90s. The Home serves women with addiction challenges.)

She went on, "It's no easier now. My dad couldn't take me to the hospital because he was at home with a catheter attached. He's supposed to remove it tomorrow himself. My mother has Alzheimer's."

We arrived at her dad's house. Her sister was waiting outside, smoking a cigarette. She barely moved to help us as I tried to maneuver my rider into the house.

"Get the wheelchair for me," she asked her sister. Her sister brought a walker. But, as I mentioned before, my rider couldn't walk. Finally, my rider convinced her to get the wheelchair. Now, the dad appeared. The mother had been on the couch smiling at me since we entered.

"Who are you?" the dad demanded.

Someone told him I'm the Uber driver.

"Oh, well, hi," he said.

Finally, everyone seemed to settle in.

I was ready to call it a night. Too many things flashed through my mind in too short a time.

One vision has been hard to erase. I'll let you guess which one.

"TRIPLE-PLAY!"

No two people have the same fingerprints. Nor do they have the same personalities or life experiences. Since driving for Uber, I've never encountered two exact copies of riders.

On one night that week, I had three very memorable riders. They spanned three generations. Keep in mind that the vast majority of my interactions with riders are cordial and pleasant. Sprinkled amidst those average rides that week were three very unique individuals.

The first was an older woman I'd Ubered at least once before. She was waiting for me outside of Walgreens. She was using a walker. I popped the hatchback, opened her door, and placed her walker in the rear of my car.

"Thank you for helping me with the walker," she said. "You're much nicer than an Uber driver I had this morning!"

"I'm sorry to hear that," I responded. "Tell me what happened."

"When the driver arrived, he popped the trunk to his car. He didn't get out; he just rolled down his window and told me to put it in the trunk. He had one of those mesh nets covering the space. I struggled to get it in, but it was too difficult. 'Can you help me with this?' I asked him. 'I have a bad neck,' he said. 'You should have told Uber that you needed special help before you asked for a ride.'"

By this time, she told me she was disgusted with the driver. She struggled to untangle her walker from the netting. Finally, she freed it and told the driver he could go away.

As an employee of the Little Sisters of the Poor nursing home, I cannot tell you how disgusted and sad her story was to me. She was a lovely woman, and the dang walker was not heavy.

* * *

A couple of rides later, I arrived at a local pub. It was still light outside. My rider was waiting for me and staggered toward my car. He was in his mid-50s.

"How's your day going?" I asked.

"Bout the same as every other day," he said. "Just turned 58 recently. Ain't got too much time left on this earth. My parents only made it to their early 60s, so I figure that's about my limit."

"Is there any reason you don't think you can go longer?" I said.

"Don't want to last longer. I've got a couple of grandkids I love, but I don't get along with my daughter all that well. They're all living with me until they finish building their house."

We arrived at his home. He looked out the window. "Well, that's not good. She's home. I'll have to go to the other side of the house. They have their own entrance."

He slowly exited the car. He stumbled toward the house. He was not very quiet for someone trying to sneak into his own home.

It saddened me to think about someone who had reached his age and had no desire to fight. I heard a priest one time say that sometimes it's more important to pray to have the desire to have the desire rather than have the thing itself. I think that's appropriate here.

* * *

The night was not over, however. The most intriguing ride was ahead.

He was waiting in front of the mall. I'd given him a ride before. Uber estimated the ride to take a little over an hour this time.

Now, I admit I'm usually the most talkative person around most people, but I never had a chance with this gentleman.

He told me he had taken an Uber from Biloxi to the mall

to buy shoes. Shoes were his livelihood. He sold specialty shoe treatments that made old shoes look brand new. He also clarified that nobody was better at sales than he was.

"I can make a thousand dollars in one day when I'm at the right place. I know sales! Nobody's better!"

I must be related to the young gentleman. Almost every sentence began with the phrase, 'Bro!' The other sentences started with the 'n-word,' a quick apology, and the insertion of 'Bro' to replace the verbal slip.

On the rare occasion when he took a breath, I asked pertinent questions. So, here's the gist of his story.

He was twenty-eight years old. He had spent seven years in prison and had been out for the last two years. He described his time in prison as a learning experience.

For a dollar an hour, he learned firefighting and the dairy business.

"I may have only made a dollar an hour, but I saved many lives while we fought huge forest fires. Bro, I made a difference! You gotta feel good about that! We were so exhausted one night that we fell asleep on the mountain. We were awakened by a burning tree that landed twenty feet away. "

He spent more time telling me about his work with dairy cows. His favorite task was herding.

"*N-word*, I mean, bro, those cows get to know you. You develop a relationship once you've moved them through the seven-minute shower and placed them in position. They'll give you the 'side-eye' if they don't trust you. I've also learned to recognize when they are not happy. Those mamas can kick the *s%^&* out of you!"

We were both laughing.

Finally, we arrived at our destination! I was exhausted but thoroughly entertained. You meet all kinds of folks when you Uber.

"THE SUN ALSO RISES!"

Ecclesiastes, Ernest Hemingway's book, and my blog. Name three places where you can find today's title phrase. Ok, the other two places are slightly more famous, but I love the sentiment.

When I started driving for Uber, I often drove until the early morning hours. Usually, I was home before sunrise. One of my evening shifts lasted through the onset of daylight.

I was approaching 11:00 PM on Friday when I got a ding to pick up a couple of Hispanic gentlemen at the Mobile Airport. They had missed their flight and were trying to book a flight from the Biloxi-Gulfport airport.

"We're booked on a flight, but we have a problem. We're returning to our hotel to grab a couple of hours of sleep. Is there any way you can pick us up there at 2:30 AM?" he asked. "We'll make it worth your while!"

"I'll make it happen!" I said.

I drove home, hopped into bed, took a short nap, and took a wake-up shower. Depending on your point of view, that qualified as my latest or earliest pickup ever. They were very grateful and kept their promise with a nice tip.

* * *

Now I had to drive back to Mobile. I was wide awake, so I might as well see if I could get more rides. Ding! I got one!

It was still dark, but someone needed a ride from downtown Mobile's McDonald's on Government Street. When I arrived, I saw a couple changing a tire in the parking lot. The young lady hopped into my car.

"He's just about finished changing the tire. I need to get home. My car is at a bar. I'm smart enough to know I didn't need to drive," she explained. "I manage one of the locations at our family business, and I have to be at work at 11:00."

I knew that was going to be a rough day for her. She slept until we reached her destination. She assured me she was close to home and had stopped drinking several hours before. The sun rose as we made the drive.

Substantially more people enjoy sunsets than experience sunrises. Both events can be stunning.

My wife and I enjoy the sunsets from our loft balcony on Dauphin Street. As you face west, the sun changes the lighting throughout downtown and finally sinks below the buildings. The street lights become more prominent, and our streets begin welcoming guests most nights. As we sit on the balcony, passersby carry on conversations without regard to listeners.

But, as the title says, *'The Sun Also Rises.'*

My wife, Lane, and I thought we would try life as Downtown residents for a year. We'd been there almost eight years. Most people around here who talk about sunsets think about a beach or mountains. I think about sunrises and the Mobile River.

A few years ago, I lost weight before our twin daughters married at the Cathedral Basilica, which was just a few months apart. My routine included rising at 5:00 AM and running in the dark through the streets of Downtown Mobile.

My route started on Dauphin Street and proceeded to the parking garage on the river. If I timed it right, I would reach the river just as the sun began to rise. The sky displayed a dazzling variety of hues, especially on partially cloudy mornings. More than once, I saw porpoises swimming up the river.

Breathtaking!

I wasn't the only one enjoying those mornings. So many other walkers and runners shared the road and pleasant waves. 'Good morning!' really meant something to them.

It wasn't always smooth, however. One morning, as I approached the Convention Center parking lot, I was blocked by a train. Instead of crossing Water Street, I took a quick right onto the sidewalk. It was still dark, so I didn't notice the graded walkway ahead.

I stumbled—very awkwardly. My arms windmilled as I tried to regain my balance. Then, the sidewalk won. Several portions of skin attached themselves to the cement. I was out of breath and lay there until I could continue my journey. I took a shortcut home.

I once attended a meeting hosted by the Mobile Police Department. They told us that there are cameras everywhere in downtown Mobile. I hope they enjoyed the show.

Not too long after, I performed another acrobatic pavement pasting on St. Louis Street again in the early morning. It took a few minutes to regain my composure, but I decided to run the last quarter-mile. I saw an elderly lady walking her dog toward me. As we got closer, she nervously crossed to the other side of the road.

I wondered why she did that when I looked down and saw a stream of blood running from my knee to my sock. Also, my white shirt was splattered with blood. I didn't blame her.

Life occurs at all hours of the day and night in my neighborhood. Sometimes, it annoys. Most of the time, we enjoy the show provided by people from all walks of life right in front of our home.

Some people in Baldwin County will tell you constantly about the sunsets on the eastern shores of Mobile Bay. And they are beautiful.

I like to think of those early morning runs along the Mobile River.

As the title says, '*The Sun Also Rises!*'

CHAPTER 6
WORLDLY

AROUND THE WORLD—
56 COUNTRIES IN 730 DAYS!

Very soon after I started driving for Uber and Lyft, I noticed a few different accents from my riders. (I don't know why, but many riders seem to think I have an accent?)

As we rode, I asked, "Where are you from?" I was genuinely amazed at the folks visiting Mobile, Alabama, from all over the planet.

One of the things I do as I drive is to listen to interesting stories or interesting people. I use an audio journal immediately after I drop off my riders to remember their 'situations' for later.

While I notice apparent differences in different cultures, the universal similarities in people from drastically different backgrounds keep returning to me. Family and close personal relationships are at the top of those universal commonalities. The desire to help others in need is also important to many of my passengers. I am also learning how to discuss differences of opinion without insulting or putting down the other person. It has taken me most of my life to learn the art of listening.

For example, I drove to one of the shipping company sites and picked up a lady from Kazakhstan and a gentleman from Turkey. We discussed geopolitical interests, especially the gentleman's expectations of the places he had visited worldwide. Specifically, he discussed a recent trip he made to Africa. He expected to see so many amazing things, especially those he viewed online, on television, and in movies. Instead, he came away disturbed by the poverty level among the general population and the obvious corruption in the various African governments.

His concern with the American population was that, in his perception, the middle and upper classes had it too easy. He seemed to believe that we were oblivious to the plight of people experiencing poverty around us. I respectfully disagreed and used my lifetime of experience working with charitable groups and my job as Development Director for the Little Sisters of the Poor to counter his view.

I explained to him that one group I belonged to, *The Rotary Club,* was greatly responsible for nearly eradicating polio worldwide. I'd been blessed to serve with so many caring people. I told him I couldn't ignore the passion I'd witnessed in those people. I think they eventually believed me, or they're still adding 'charity' to politics and religion as subjects to avoid with strangers.

* * *

Sometimes, I get a story that is a little 'different.' I received a 'ding' from near the University of South Alabama. He was a student from Kuwait, one of dozens I transport around Mobile. He told me that he had recently taken in a cat.

He said, "Both of us are suffering from fleas. I can't seem to get them out of my apartment."

He continued, "That's not my biggest problem, though. I'm suffering from impending baldness, and as you seem to have most of your hair at your advanced age, I was hoping you have a suggestion for a remedy. I have had some success with Rogaine, but I'm still worried about going bald!"

Even at my 'advanced' age, I'm not sure I provided any help besides an ear. I had concerns about his 'other' problem and spent the next few hours checking my car for fleas.

Incomprehensible!

Sometimes (often), you pick up riders who can't communicate well because of clarity-inhibiting liquid refreshments. Other times, it's because of extreme foreign accents or the inability to speak English at all. In those two years of Ubering, I had picked up riders from fifty-seven foreign countries.

'Ding!' My app showed a request from someone dining at Felix's on the Causeway, my favorite seafood restaurant, and their impeccable service. As I pulled up out front, two Japanese gentlemen entered my vehicle. They both worked at the steel plant just north of Mobile.

They tried to carry on a conversation with me, but the combination of alcohol and accent made it nearly impossible. Whatever answers I gave to their questions, they would repeat them to each other and then switch to Japanese. After the Japanese part of the conversation, they would begin laughing hysterically.

One of the few things I could get out of them was that the gentleman in the front seat was the mentor for the one in the back. Virtually every question and answer spoken in English came from the mentor.

I was a little self-conscious, but every time they laughed, I laughed along with them. Overall, though, they were a lot of fun and seemed to enjoy themselves.

* * *

Fast-forward a couple of days, and I got another *'ding'* to pick up riders at another great restaurant, the Blue Gill, on the Causeway. This time, it was four Japanese gentlemen. The three youngest ones sat in the back seat. The guy who sat in the front seat was the gentleman who rode in the back seat two nights before.

He greeted me, "Oh, Mr. Tommy...so sorry about the other night!" He shook my hand and said something to the guys in the back seat.

They laughed.

I told him, "No problem, we had a great time. No need to apologize."

They would crack up after he spoke in Japanese to the guys in the back. He would turn back to me each time, shake my hand, and say, "So sorry about the other night!" He did this several times.

That was when I decided to do something I had never done before or since. I recorded them. There was a Japanese lady who worked at the Little Sisters of the Poor, my daytime job, who I thought might translate for me.

Again, I dropped them off at their destination and received a nice tip and a *'Thanks for a great time!'* response.

Unfortunately, the next day, my translator said all she could understand was that they were drunk and talked over each other so much she couldn't understand what they were saying. I was still suspicious. She was such a nice person. She probably didn't want to hurt my feelings.

Sometimes, the challenge to understand is not caused by alcohol or a foreign language. I picked up a young Asian woman who could not hear and, as far as I could tell, could not speak.

Sitting in my car, she showed me a note on her phone that said, "Please take me to Walmart, then please wait for me so I can have a ride back."

She assured me that she would not be very long. After waiting more than twenty-five minutes, I got out of my car, approached the doors, and saw her coming with a basket full of groceries and other items.

When she got into the car, I assumed she wanted to return to the house where we started. I was wrong. When we arrived there, she communicated to me that she had not put the ending address on the app and started waving her arms wildly to indicate where I was to turn. The problem was that I had to constantly look at her gyrations behind me while simultaneously watching the road ahead.

We finally arrived at the proper destination. I was a nervous wreck. I was until I realized how challenging it must be for her in her daily life.

* * *

Sometimes, it's just downright funny. I picked up five large guys working on ships serviced in our area. They were at Longhorn Steakhouse and wanted to go to Lucky's Irish Pub on Airport Blvd.

Because of their pronounced accent, I asked where they were from.

One said, "I'm from Scotland, he's from Scotland, he's from Ireland, he's from Romania, and he's from Scotland."

The accents were hilarious, especially the guy from Romania.

I usually don't like to hear a lot of the *'F' word* flying around, but I must admit I was laughing hysterically listening to all these guys talking about each other. The 'F' word was loudly and lavishly sprinkled throughout.

The Romanian was upset that he couldn't get his debit card to work here at these ATMs.

One kept telling him, "You're not supposed to type your license number into the ATM."

The abuse was equally spread among all nationalities! I couldn't pick a winner. Hilarious!

FOREIGN AFFAIRS

I had now had more than 9,000 rides and driven folks from at least sixty-seven countries.

It was a new milestone—more than 3,900 rides and folks from at least 60 countries! You can usually expect an average of at least two passengers per ride, so I had almost 8,000 people in my car. I am still amazed at the folks worldwide who visit Mobile for so many different reasons.

I got dinged one evening by two Japanese gentlemen. Only one of them spoke English. He asked me, "Can you recommend some foreign restaurants in Mobile?"

I was taking them to a Nepal/Indian restaurant called Katmandu. I started naming as many 'foreign' restaurants as I could remember. (Is Taco Bell a foreign restaurant?)

"No, No!" he said. "Not your foreign restaurants. Our foreign restaurants! Southern food!"

Well, that's quite a different thing!

When I dropped them off, they asked for my phone number because they wanted to call their 'taxi' when they were ready to go somewhere else. It usually didn't work that way, but I 'taxied' them a few more places that night.

* * *

A few weeks later, I picked up a young man who was originally from Lithuania. He was traveling with a young lady who hardly opened her mouth. They were eventually traveling to New Orleans, but I took them to Pensacola. No, I was not disoriented. The guy was a salesperson for Vivint, selling home security systems throughout the Gulf Coast to work his way through college. He had been accepted to Stanford but would be attending BYU soon.

He was one of three adoptees in his family and one of eight kids in total. Somehow, he was part Native American from

Arizona but didn't know much about the details. I think some connections there initially brought him to the United States.

He told me, "I spent the first eight years of my life in foster homes, the last three with my eventual adoptive parents."

He said he was very close to his adoptive parents but didn't have a close relationship with the five original children because they had grown up and left by the time of the three adoptions. His goal was to work his way through college without accumulating any debt. I didn't have any doubt that he would be successful!

* * *

Language can often become a challenge. I picked up a French couple living just outside Paris on this particular ride. My Uber map was a little stubborn, so it wasn't showing me their destination.

She told me they were going to a wedding at '*fockundee.*' If there was some way to type the extreme accent, you might understand my confusion after asking her 3-4 times to repeat herself. Eventually, I realized she was going to "Fort Conde!"

They told me they loved the friendliness of people in Mobile. I'd heard that so many times from people outside of our area. I had to wonder. It doesn't seem like we're acting any different than we do all the time. I love that about my hometown!

All of these international experiences aren't always pleasant.

* * *

One late night, I picked up a Saudi Arabian gentleman who had been in Mobile earning a college degree for the last six years. He asked me to take him to an ATM because he was leaving at 4:00 am the following day. He also told me that his girlfriend had just ended their relationship before she knew he was leaving to go home.

He was very upset with her but would leave her the TV, couch, and other items. The conversation got a little crazy at that point.

"Americans are not generous! That is why I'm leaving the TV and couch with her! That will teach her a lesson!"

I tried countering the generosity point. I had no idea what his lesson was supposed to teach his ex-girlfriend. I explained my work with the Little Sisters of the Poor and the multitudes of charitable groups nationwide. I honestly believe the people of this country are the most generous in the world.

He said, "Well, some are good. You're older and wiser! The rest of these (expletives deleted) are BS!"

Furthermore, he shouted, "She never appreciated the fact that I paid my girlfriend's rent several times, bought Jack Daniels for her Dad, and provided 'weed' for her Mom!" (Kind of a bizarre vision of charity, don't you think?)

Thankfully, we finally reached the destination.

I've never said these rides were boring!

"INTERNATIONAL ENCOUNTER!"

I picked him up outside of a West Mobile bar. He appeared to be in his early thirties and had obviously been in the establishment for more than a few minutes. The word 'cordial' came to my mind as we began small talk. Friendly, but the verbiage was a little disjointed at times.

"My family is from Tibet," he said. "We've been in Mobile since I was in my teens."

He asked, "Would you mind stopping at this Chinese takeout restaurant on the way to my house? I need to pick up some dinner for my wife and me."

I was happy to oblige. We don't make much money from waiting, but most riders are glad to add a tip, so I was not worried about the wait.

I could see through the window that he was about 3rd or 4th in line. A few minutes later, his turn came.

I saw him gesturing to the cook, bypassing the counter employee. The cook nodded, then returned to the stove. Now, my Tibetan rider began gesturing a little more forcefully. The cook returned to the counter and gestured back. Not only were those two beginning to show frustration, but the other customers seemed to be getting involved. From my point of view, it appeared that the mob had appointed a spokesman, who now seemed to be translating.

These 'negotiations' continued for about two hours. (Truthfully, it may have been more like five or ten minutes, but you've been there, right?). Eventually, another customer left the restaurant.

As he passed my car, I asked him, "That's my rider in there. Any idea what's going on?"

He laughed and said, "Neither seems to understand what the other is saying. The owner/cook speaks English, but not all that well. The customer was trying to order seafood for his wife, who is on a paleo diet. The cook thought the guy wanted the fried seafood with no butter or oil. Each time the guy explained it to him, he pointed out that you can't fry the shrimp without butter or oil.

"Finally, another guy in line figures it out," he continued. "The 'drunk' guy wanted him to cook the shrimp without **batter.** With his slur, it comes out sounding like butter. The lady working the counter was confusing it even further."

A few minutes later, my rider returned to the car and apologized. As we continued to his home, he told me he had worked in his Dad's business at some point. I told him I'd published a book about conflicts in our family business. It turned out that we have mutual acquaintances.

When we got to his house, he insisted I sell him a copy of my book, and we stood in the front yard talking as a light rain began to fall.

I mistakenly asked him what he wanted to do with his life since he seemed to want to move on to a new career. He began with some background. We moved under my raised hatchback to protect ourselves from the drizzle.

He described the changes in Tibet that led his parents to flee to the United States after China re-established rule in the early 1950's. Finally, he told me that his goal was to visit Bhutan. He told me that there was no crime at all in Bhutan.

"However," he said, "for some reason, divorce is a major problem there."

I wonder if the guys in Bhutan have as much of a challenge delivering their wife's dinner?

Just saying!?

"A WORLD APART!"

Friday nights are my best, well, most interesting Uber nights. That Friday was no different. The time goes by faster when it's busy. This was a busy night!

Sometime around 12:30 am, Saturday morning, I was summoned to the Walmart Superstore. When I arrived, I saw a group of folks with their purchases standing out front. They seemed to be trying to determine who would ride in my car.

"How many of you are going?" I asked. (I'm an UberXL, which usually means a maximum of six passengers).

A gentleman with a very noticeable British accent leaned in the passenger window. "I'm from the UK. We only have one phone with the Uber app. Can you call another taxi for us? We can pay cash!"

That's not really how this works, so we just looked at each other.

He finally asked, "Can we try to fit eight of us in there? Otherwise, we can't get everyone back to the ship."

So, we gave it a try.

Once all eight were in the vehicle with their packages, we started. It was about a 34-minute trip. I noticed some very 'non-British' conversations.

I asked, "Where is everyone from?"

"I'm from the UK. We've got four from Romania, two from India, and one from Malaysia."

What an interesting bunch of folks. I'd taken folks from 64 different countries, which had been a fascinating part of this venture. There was so much laughter and fun among these folks. Once we unpacked everyone, they could not have been more grateful.

* * *

The next ride was different. A world apart!

Uber dispatched me to a trailer park in Theodore. It was shortly after 2:00 am, Saturday morning. The app said I was to pick up John. I didn't see anyone, so I called.

John answered, "I see you...just keep coming. I'm walking toward you."

He said, "You'll be giving my brother a ride to the Greyhound Bus Station. He's coming down the road just ahead." Then, he walked away.

I saw the brother walking toward me. He was holding a trash bag with a couple of blankets, a half-packed overnight bag, and a small dog. We loaded his 'luggage' in the rear.

"How's your night going?" I ask.

"I've had better," he answered. "I guess I'm heading back to California. My brother and I just had it out! I wasn't happy with our arrangement, so I told him so, and he took that as an ultimatum. I had given up my Social Security in California to come back here with him. He told me he could get me a job drilling and help me with a place to live."

I tried to determine his age. I guessed that he was in his forties. I asked him what had happened.

"The job at the drilling platform didn't work out. That's when my brother said he would pay me to stay in a trailer and care for his five pit bulls. He never paid me. That's why I gave him what he called an ultimatum. I told him that if he wasn't going to pay me..." he trailed off.

He went on again, "I need cash. I had no money of my own; I would have to go back to California. He responded that he would give me a start right now, but only as far as the bus station. That's when you showed up."

I had to ask. "What happened to the drilling job?"

"They fired me for drugs. Marijuana. I think my brother set

me up. We drink the same beer and smoke the same weed. When we were called in for a drug test, he told me to drink this liquid, and it would mask the marijuana. It didn't work. I found out that he had some synthetic urine that he hid in his pants just for that purpose. He passed his test and kept his job. That's when he told me I could stay here and take care of his pit bulls."

He continued, "I have a license to smoke in California, but they don't allow that here in Louisiana."

I said, "They don't allow that here in Alabama either."

He said, "Ever since I got here in Louisiana, it's been nothing but trouble. I love my brother, but I think he did me wrong. Now I've got to go back to California. The way he treated my dog and me was wrong. Treating me wrong is one thing, but my dog is my only friend."

We were approaching the Greyhound station.

I asked him, "How are you going to get from here to California?"

"I don't know. Somehow, I guess. I don't have any money for the bus or anything, but I'll start here and see what happens."

I told him I would pray for him. At this point, he didn't even seem sure that he wanted to go back. He was just stuck.

"Thank you for praying for me. I do believe in God, and I know I have to change. Maybe this will be a start for me and my dog?"

Thanks again for following these stories. These experiences with people from all over the world and all aspects of life's challenges have been enlightening. It has strengthened my gratitude for the blessings of my family and friends.

God has been very good to me.

"POV!"

"I had no idea Mobile was such a beautiful town!" he said. "I bet these homes must be expensive!"

I love taking riders along Government Blvd. or Dauphin Street, especially when the sun sets or rises. The point of view (POV) shows our historic homes in their best light. That's a very different perception than the heavy traffic many visitors see as they travel from the Mobile Regional Airport.

Of course, different people hold different views based on their prior experiences or their current attitudes.

* * *

That week, I answered the Uber ding to pick up riders at the WalMart Supercenter on the Beltline. After loading their purchases in the back, we began our ride toward their ship docked at Ezra Trice Blvd., Мобил, Алабама.

The rider's name was in the same hieroglyphic lettering used for my hometown above.

"How do you pronounce your name?" I asked.

"Most people call me Alex. We're from Ukraine. We work on the ship," he said.

I'd picked up more than a few Ukrainians passing through Mobile. I know I'm not the only one wondering why they're not at home defending their homeland. So, I asked, "How is your family handling the war back home?"

"We escaped to Greece after we lost everything at home. We lived in four houses between my family, my wife's family, brothers and sisters, and their families. Now, all of us are living in one house. It's tough, but we had nowhere else to go.

"If we had waited any longer," he continued, "our families would have been separated, and the men forced to serve in the military.

"I make enough money on the ships to care for my family. There is no way I could have done that if I stayed."

I wondered what he thought the future would look like for Ukraine based on who ultimately 'won' the war.

"It's a disaster," he said. "If Russia wins, it's a disaster. If Ukraine wins, it will be a disaster. We have nothing to go back to either way."

"How are the Greek people treating you?" I asked.

"They are wonderful. We know they are challenged, but they've been very welcoming to us. America has also been a blessing, but it's too expensive for us to move here.

"I have no past beyond the last two years. We have no pictures, no records, nothing from our life in Ukraine. My only pictures are those I've taken on my phone in the last two years."

My riders were grateful to have the chance to form new lives with their families and loved ones. That was quite an interesting point of view.

* * *

Later that same evening, I picked up a couple on Royal Street in downtown Mobile. I greeted them in my customary manner. "How's your evening going?"

"This is one of the worst days of my life!" said the gentleman. "Nothing has gone right all day!"

Okay, I thought, *let's see where this goes.* "So, what's happening to make it so bad?"

"We've been awake for twenty hours because your port officials require us to be escorted to the front gate to leave. It took more than an hour and a half to get transportation to the front entrance.

"We haven't eaten all day, and we came to this restaurant on Royal Street, and they wouldn't even let her in to eat just because she's nineteen. I'm 31, so I could eat, but that doesn't help."

(Apparently, I've now opened the spigot!)

"In most ports, I can buy alcohol to take on the ship. But I'm not allowed to do that here. Now I'm tired, hungry, can't get any liquor to enjoy, and have to be back at the shipyard in two hours. We never have this problem in New Orleans."

He was not finished. "I guess when we get to Walmart, I'll buy a case of beer and take it on the ship. If I can't get that through, they can keep it!"

His accent told me he was from a different country, so I asked, "Where are you from?"

"We're from Greece!" he said.

"That's interesting," I told him. "Earlier tonight, I picked up two gentlemen from Ukraine who escaped with their families to Greece. They said your country's hospitality blessed them."

No response.

He waited a few minutes, looked around, and said, "There's another thing I don't understand about Americans. There are too many homes for one family here. I can't imagine how lonely it must be to be so separated from other people."

"We live in large apartment buildings. We're welcomed by lots of people when we come home, and there are always others nearby to live with. It seems more friendly than living in your own 'castle' or whatever people think they're doing."

Thankfully, we arrived at Walmart.

"Well, I hope this is your worst day for a while. It sounds like things have to get better. Have a good evening!" I told them.

"Thanks for the ride. It has to get better."

POV. Your point of view does matter.

CHAPTER 7
MY THOUGHTS

ALL IN THE FAMILY

I've spent most of my life in a family business. However, my first 'real' job was not with my family business. A friend's dad was the manager at the Bama Drive-In Theatre. Most readers have never experienced parking their car beside a pole with a speaker attached. Remove the speaker, pull it into your window, peer through the windshield, and view the giant screen, often a half-football field away.

That job paid $5.00 per night. We were tasked with serving popcorn, hot dogs, fountain drinks, and more to families, including pajama-clad kids and 16-year-olds who created enough steam inside their vehicles to power a small paddle-wheeler.

That job lasted about two months for me. I soon upgraded to our family business and a 40-hour-a-week summer job, bringing in $1.00/hour!

For the next forty-some-odd years, my experience in that family-owned business affected everything in my life.

This is why my ears perk up whenever a rider talks about a family business. Ride-sharing has also taught me that appearances are not always what they seem.

I answered the call to pick up a rider at In-Town Suites. As I approached, I saw a heavily tattooed and pierced young man. He worked for his dad's contracting company. We were about 45 minutes from our destination, which gave us plenty of time to talk.

"We plan that when my dad passes away, the business will be left to my stepmother," he said. "At that point, she expects to call on him to take over the business immediately."

Alarm bells were going off in my head! This was a recipe for disaster. As our ride ended, I gave him my book, '*An Act of Congress—The Real-Life Story of Power and Politics in Family Business*,' and a copy of '*Every Family's Business*' by

Thomas Deans. He, his dad, and his stepmom had a lot of discussion time ahead.

* * *

A few weeks later, I picked up a young man working with his father, running an oriental restaurant in town. He was so enthusiastic about the future! His father had been sharing ownership with him. You could tell he took pride in being a co-owner. I had so many questions, but our ride was too short. I gave him my phone number in case he had any questions.

Unfortunately, I drove by their place a few months later. They were closed. I would love to know the story.

* * *

Once again, appearances are deceiving, as I picked up a young white man sporting a Rastafarian/dreadlock hairstyle. He told me he piloted a small plane nationwide, taking aerial photos for real estate companies and government entities. He had also worked for a family-owned business teaching people how to fly.

"Dad owns the business. My younger brother and I worked there until recently. To pay off my student loans, I left the company and took a job with an aerial photography company. Dad's pretty upset with me."

I asked, "Do you think you will ever go back into the family business?"

He said, "My brother still works there on the mechanical side of the business. He and I have discussed that whenever Dad turns the business over to my brother, my brother has promised to invite me back to run the administrative side of the company. We're both hopeful that Dad will accept our plan in time," he concluded.

He also got a copy of my book and the one by Thomas Deans.

It's uncanny how easy it is for me to see massive calamity ahead for these folks. I know what it's like to think things will 'work out.' It takes much more than wishing. It takes 'that' talk. And, it's not just family businesses; it is true in any relationship.

Please don't make your desires secret, whether it's family business succession or who gets Aunt Carolyn's knitting collection. The earlier everyone expresses themselves, the easier the conversation goes.

Plan ahead and write it down!!

WHAT'S ON TONIGHT?

What would it feel like if you could sit in front of your television with your favorite beverage and popcorn and watch your life portrayed by actors? What if those actors gave you several versions of how those moments may have played out?

That's how I envision so many conversations in my car as I take passengers to their destination via ride-sharing. It might happen in direct exchanges, or it may be that I overhear them. I could play out entire episodes I've overheard in phone discussions. (If you think I shouldn't 'listen' in, you may be correct, but it's not practical. If you want a private conversation, do it in private. Besides, I need the entertainment!)

The other night, I picked up a father and his seven-year-old daughter at a restaurant on the Causeway. They were enjoying a father-daughter date. As I sat in my recliner, munching on popcorn (figuratively), I saw myself in two roles. One role brought back memories of being a child and telling my mom or dad about things that happened at school or playing in the neighborhood. My dad worked several jobs besides being an air traffic controller, so I felt that I had to spill my guts in short order to catch him up on my experiences.

Or, as I sat watching the scenario, I could put myself in the place of the dad. He was his daughter's soccer coach and was in his third year. I have coached 18 of my kid's sports teams over the years. All the dad had to say was, "Tell Mr. Tommy (a name I'm often called by younger folks and those familiar with this quaint Southern custom) what happened at your last soccer game!"

The little girl immediately recounted the moments that led to her scoring a goal to tie the game in the last few seconds. It made no difference to her that her team lost in a shootout. You could appreciate the pride of her dad.

I had so many opportunities to live that out with my five

kids. Sports can be such a positive part of life. I've also had riders demonstrate the negative side of the ledger, which most kids' sports attendees have witnessed. I picked up a gentleman who was on his phone when he entered my car and remained so until he exited. He was the perfect combination of Southern efficiency and Northern charm.

The gist of his phone discussion had to do with sportsmanship. At the end of the game, he was discussing (in a loud voice, I must add) that he excoriated the parents of his son's teammates for not walking across the field to shake the hands of the victors. The opponents were so excited that they were busy celebrating, so his son was the only player to cross the field to congratulate the winners. He lamented that because he was from a small rural town and not part of the 'elite' here, he had always been taught to win or lose gracefully.

I can't tell you how many times I saw perfectly well-mannered folks lose their mind around kid's sports. Most of the parents and coaches I had been around were role models for our local society. I saw more kids with the attitude of the seven-year-old than the other kind.

Further into the 'show,' I saw scenes of college kids acting like there is nothing else in the world outside of their own entertainment and self-importance. I want to say that I never had those moments, but too many of my contemporaries were eyewitnesses, if not also participants. I'm so glad that there is an alternative to the 'designated driver' policy we pretended to use when I was that young (stupid). From 'over-imbibing' to breakup emotions and everything in between, I've seen and heard these episodes through several generations. It's interesting, as I watch these shows in my car, that nothing really has changed over all these decades.

I've enjoyed seeing these next episodes. These are the ones when half of those mentioned above are married, almost all have started jobs or careers, and some are beginning to raise children. I've picked up large groups of these later twenty-year-olds several times, only to give them rides separately later.

The first wave comprises the new parents, who recognize that the babysitter needs to go home and that the baby(ies) do not care at all what time their parents got home, nor what shape they were in. They will rise very early and will not moderate their morning activities.

Next week, I'll continue this series. Isn't that the way the entertainment industry produces its shows nowadays? There is a point that I'm getting to with this, but I will have to finish that in the next issue. From the thirties to the forties, fifties, and further, the sequels will introduce us to moments that will pull together our own quilt. But make no mistake, we will all pull fabric from the same bolts. The pieces come together in a different order so that each of our lives is unique; the squares are placed in various patterns. Some make sense. Some look like they were thrown together haphazardly.

I have a special feeling for these mosaics of life as I spend each day at the Sacred Heart Residence of the Little Sisters of the Poor. I want to touch on this part of life in subsequent issues. Some of these beautiful people have lived a decade or decades, and many have lived just a decade or so less. Many are still adding colors to their patterns, just as older parts are beginning to fade.

P.S.— To the brother and sister I had the pleasure of driving with for four hours tonight...you are in my prayers and the Men of St. Joseph's intentions. Your faith in God through your trials and tribulations is terrific! Keep hoping!

WHAT'S ON TONIGHT? — PART 2

That week, I pondered what it would be like to sit in front of your TV and watch actors portray the moments of your life.

The point is that throughout the last two and a half years, I've seen my riders living out so many episodes of my life. If I haven't experienced their moments, I've been close enough to see them live out around me.

When you think you've lived a unique life, and truthfully, we all have, you see others going through similar encounters. The interesting part is seeing how people approach these challenges, losses, and victories. Each time I pick up passengers, a new show begins!

We have already discussed much of the first third or so of life in the previous column. We've all shared similar moments from childhood to those awkward teenage years, from the early twenties to adulthood. In the last chapter, we left off with the experience of becoming a parent and the tremendous responsibility of raising children. Or transitioning from job to job as we try to determine our future direction.

It's the 'short' stories that give me insight. One evening, I picked up a young traveling male nurse. He loved having temporary locations, usually lasting six months to a year. The demand was so high around the country that he had been able to 'taste' different cultures.

He told me a story about a restaurant in Minot, ND, that featured a periodic 'Grandmother's' night. This was a series of six to eight grandmothers who would cook their 'special' family meals for the public at this restaurant. These women constantly drew the largest crowds.

* * *

I picked up a 'forty-something' African-American insurance

attorney one Wednesday night. He was in town for just one night but asked me to take him to a bible study on Holcombe Avenue that he had found out about. The next day, he settled a claim and returned to Houston. He said, "No matter where I go, I try to find the opportunity to study God's word. It's amazing to see the variety of ways so many people approach the Bible. That's how I choose to spend my 'spare' time."

I've spent much of my life in a family business. Most of that experience was wonderful and formed a significant part of my identity. We all have to overcome failures in our lives, and my biggest regret is that I couldn't solve our puzzle as our third-generation business faded into oblivion. I've spent years studying the dynamics of family businesses, including earning a designation at one time as an advisor at Family Firm Institute. As I return to the theme of this chapter, *watching actors live out parts of your life,* my rider's discussions about their family businesses are my favorite.

One of the better models I've seen came from a rider attending a family business retreat for their 'foundation' annual meeting. The foundation is the family business. My rider explained that she was part of the company's third generation, which consisted of 14 'kids.' She and her siblings made up half of that generation. That means she is 1/7th of 1/3rd of the total. There were three families in the 2nd generation who initially split the ownership. The foundation aimed to invest mainly in start-ups and new entrepreneurial ventures. To invest or declare dividends, they must have the support of the majority of the 14 owners. They had hired a professional family business advisor, which has worked well for them all.

As I continued watching this 'program,' I saw the changes in the generations and the differences in their priorities. Many of the parents I meet are trying desperately to get their child/children to leave and go out into the world. Some of those 'kids' graduated from college two or three years ago. Many of these families will reverse their roles a decade or so later. As the parents grow older, many of them cannot care for themselves.

* * *

It's an old saying, but still a truism. '*You reap what you sow!*'

I picked up two couples from a restaurant on the Causeway. They were lively discussing one's father and the havoc he was causing them at home. He could no longer live alone, but he wasn't ready to go to an assisted living facility.

After some spirited but humorous stories, I asked, "Have you already decided how you want *your* kids to handle this when the time comes for you?"

There was a sudden look of horror, then laughter, then concern. They would be making a decision very soon. Their children will watch for guidance regarding their choices in a few decades.

We become the picture of all the things we do throughout our lives. Good decisions, bad decisions, patches, and fixes form the quilts we become. I've had the pleasure and honor to listen to folks who have tasted eight or nine or even more decades of life. I hope I learn from their wisdom and can offer something worthwhile to the people I come across in my life. I've had more than 8,400 people in my car in the last few years while doing this rideshare gig.

The stories I hear come from all over the planet. Sixty-one countries, plus probably every state in the United States, have been represented in my car. There is hope. We have so much in common! Once we get past the differences in perspective, we can solve the actual problems!

HUMILITY OR HUMILIATION?

I'm somewhere in the second half of my life. It has taken most of the first half, plus a few years, for me to understand the difference between humility and humiliation. The good news is that I'm rapidly approaching the age at which I can no longer be personally humiliated. That's not to say I can't cause that emotion for family and friends. But that's their problem.

Humility is another thing altogether. During the first half of my life, I was often concerned with other people's opinions of me. Folks rarely accused me of being humble. I didn't have a spot on my curriculum vitae for that information. God has a funny way of exposing parts of one's life in a way that allows us to learn... 'it ain't all about us!'

This came to mind when I picked up a group of enthusiastic realtors in Mobile for a large regional conference. I love the feeling of fun and freedom when folks are on a 'road trip' with their colleagues. This group exhibited that joviality.

One of the advantages of having a third-row seat in my Santa Fe is that it allows me to pile more folks into my car. That is also one of the disadvantages.

Once the ladies are all settled in (yes, gender diversity is not evident in this small sample), they explain that they are all affiliated with the same company but different agencies throughout the Southeast. I mentioned that I used to be a Realtor® myself.

Eschewing any semblance of humility, I stated, "Yes, I was pretty good at residential real estate and became one of the speakers for a panel that welcomed new agents for the Mobile Area Association of Realtors!"

The lady in the front passenger seat began to recruit me. "You're never too old to get back into the business!" she opined. (I'm not sure I thought I was too old until she pointed that out to me?!?)

My hearing ability on these rides amazes even me. My wife thinks I'm hard of hearing and often encourages me to get my hearing checked. She probably isn't reading this. Don't tell her I think I hear everything I want to hear. She loves me anyway!

From the third seat in the back of my car, I heard, "I hope I don't end up someday driving an Uber for a living, telling stories about how I used to be a great salesperson or some other 'past' achievement!"

OUCH!

My 'recruiter' looks at me and tries to gauge whether I heard that. I laugh and tell her I hope I don't end up that way either! About 5-10 years after hearing it, I finally understood one of life's truisms.

What other people think of me is none of my business!

I have this agreement with my maker. Someday, we'll meet, and in all humility, what He thinks of me is all that will ever matter.

In my day job, I work with Catholic nuns—the Little Sisters of the Poor. I've never seen a better definition of true humility anywhere else. These ladies take a lifetime vow of poverty, chastity, obedience, and hospitality. They dedicate their lives to caring for the elderly poor—to be there for them when transitioning from this life.

I've picked up caregivers who work with people challenged with every infirmity you can imagine. I've met people who care more deeply about their family and friends than they care about themselves. I've also picked up community leaders with proud reputations, only to have them tell me that their life is miserable. Outward appearances are not always reality.

I've been humiliated more times than I've shown humility. It may take me until I'm 100, but I will keep trying to know the difference! And even though I know the _truth,_ I still kinda care what you think of me. But it's not really any of my business.

"STATE OF MY UNION ADDRESS!"

This was my 56th blog post, now turned into a chapter for this book. I don't know what I expected when I began writing, but I'm pleased about the journey. It really is a journey! This was a week for milestones. I gave my 5,000th ride that week with Uber and Lyft. The average number of passengers was at least two, probably more. I'd had more than 10,000 people in my Hyundai Santa Fe. *10,000!*

I'd met people from 63 different countries. Most of those were here on business. Some were just passing through. Some were attending college in Mobile. Some worked on Mobile's cruise ship or in the shipyards. Some fascinating countries include Zimbabwe, Croatia, Gambia, Iceland, Nepal, Tibet, Yemen, and Vietnam. Well, all of them were interesting.

I've given rides to college students who were intelligent enough to know they needed a designated driver and those who probably should have taken the additional step of remaining at home. This level of decision-making inadequacy is unfortunately not confined to our youth. Riders of all ages have been 'poured' out of my car and escorted to their home or hotel door.

Sometimes, we ride-sharers are involved in the conversations, and sometimes we are just listeners. (You do know we can hear you, right?) We drivers can tune out much of the colorful verbiage offered from the high end of the decibel scale—just one little hint: that can be less challenging than trying to tune out whispers. I hesitate to bring this up because we drivers desire entertainment as much as the next person. The reality shows on TV pale in comparison.

I've picked up riders from prison. Others were on their way to job interviews. One rider was heading off to his third attempt at cleansing his body of opioids at a rehabilitation facility. Several times, I've been asked to counsel spouses complaining about domestic challenges. I've given life advice to hundreds of riders, sometimes unsolicited. (Most of my advice comes via mistakes I've learned through experience, often the advice I gave myself but didn't follow. Yikes!)

I'm flattered that folks younger than me, who are now most of the population, believe that I have some wisdom I can share with them. I must admit that I probably have a somewhat inflated view of myself, but they realize I'm an Uber driver, right?

* * *

I had a former college football player and his wife in my car. After I spent several minutes bragging about my wife and kids, she asked what we did to make that happen.

"We don't want to hear all that!" he said.

"We have a new child. I want to hear, so you just shut up!" she responded.

He shut up.

I explained that they accomplished their successes because that's who they are. My wife, Lane, gets the credit for a lot of that, but the ability and willingness to achieve is a decision they've made on their own. I've excelled at giving them examples of things you shouldn't do.

I've picked up folks who drive $100,000.00 Teslas and gigantic off-road vehicles. One rider told me a story of how his company — *'Rednecks with Paychecks'*—came into existence and how it presented an eye-opening experience to a British broadcaster who had a total misconception of the people who live in the South. There is a lot of that going around.

I've had some political discussions and some religious discussions from time to time. I'm not sure what those did to my ratings, but I came away from each occasion believing we could have these discussions without any injection of hate. Sometimes, we disagree on what we want, but we almost always disagree on how to reach common destinations.

One of the most rewarding aspects of ride-sharing is that my riders trigger my memories of some of the stories of my life. My wife, family, and friends have heard these stories thousands of times. I love a new audience. You may have noticed that many of the stories have nothing to do with a ride. Almost all of them were triggered by something said or done while driving.

I cannot finish this story without mentioning how special my 'regular' job at the Little Sisters of the Poor is to me. The opportunity to be with people who have lived most of their lives and accumulated such a wealth of knowledge and experience is priceless. It becomes even more special to see the dedication and love from the folks who work and volunteer their lives to the care and comfort of these precious elderly gems.

This blog is my clumsy effort to give you my "State of My Union Address." I spent those last few days reviewing my columns and realizing how much I love meeting people and sharing life with them. I especially enjoy sharing my thoughts with my readers.

"I'M BAAAACCCKKK!"

I missed y'all! I'm sure many of you are thinking, "Great! He missed us! - Who is this?"

My last blog to you was on August 24, 2021. I said I wanted to take a few months off to work on my book. Unfortunately, I took a lot of months off and have yet to write my book. So, here I am.

When I stopped writing, I had posted 113 blogs. Forty-three were Uber/Rideshare related, 33 were personal/slice-of-life oriented, and 37 were political. Is it possible to combine all three? We'll see.

I've continued to drive for Uber. At that point, I had welcomed more than 16,000 riders in my car. They'd been from at least 68 countries. They came from all walks of life. Wealthy, homeless, old, young, white-collar, blue-collar, articulate, barely understandable, and folks from every demographic.

They fascinate me!

Lots of my riders are quiet or carry on conversations with other passengers. Many of them spend their ride time with me on their phones, seemingly oblivious to my presence. And, yes, I do 'eavesdrop' on their side of the discussions. But, on the other hand, I can often hear the other side of those calls, especially when impaired by mind-altering substances. (Them, not me).

I should apologize, but really, they're in charge of their discretion. While many suspect that Alexa and Siri are secretly listening to our discussions, you can be sure that if you are saying something interesting in my car, I'm probably paying attention, too.

Some of my riders solicit interaction. I enjoy that myself. We have violated most 'polite' rules, especially those prohibiting politics and religion. Those were the most enlightening to me.

The theme I had settled on while writing these stories will remain the same. *'What Do We Really Want?'* Of course, we can discuss topics for which we disagree. But, on the other hand, I'm sure we'll have a lot of opinions in common.

I have plenty of 'Uber' stories to share with you. I look forward to your opinions, experiences, and life solutions to shared challenges. I've been away from this forum for a while, and my rustiness is showing.

"TIS OF THEE!"

I picked up a young truck driver at a Theodore truck stop. He needed a ride to a nearby Dollar General store and back.

"I'm from Morocco!" he said in an excited voice. His English was halting, but he was anxious to get his thoughts out. "No racism in America!"

I tried to make sense of that statement. He again said, "No prejudice! I have good job here! I'm Muslim. No matter. I make living here!"

I'd love to tell you that I suddenly began to understand what he was telling me. I made some effort at light conversation.

"People around here don't care that much about color or ethnicity. We prefer to judge folks by how they act first." I know that's my goal, and I think most people around here feel that way.

He was still enthusiastic when I got him back to the truck stop. "Thank you, sir! People are friendly in America! Thank you!" he said.

On that 4th of July, I was thinking about the people I'd engaged over the last six and a half years while Ubering. The young gentleman I mentioned above represented one of at least 68 countries.

Many riders were visiting the United States, and others were on business. Many folks were here permanently, hoping to make a life for themselves and their families. I won't use this column to discuss immigration politics. Maybe later.

As crazy as times seem to so many of us, I'm convinced that 99% of these people believe this is the greatest country in the world. I can't count the number of conversations from riders telling me they pray that we don't lose what made us great. That fear is rampant among our citizens.

So, are we in the best of times or the worst of times?

That's up to us. As an Uber driver, I've picked up people in the finest neighborhoods and the most dismal homes. Some riders were homeless or on the verge. Throughout that stratum, there is some uniformity. Almost everyone I've talked with thinks that we've gone too far.

They want to have clarity. We've crossed some line that makes them feel they're losing control. They seem ready to raise the bar on life standards. We're not there yet, but recognizing that we're out of whack is the first, most crucial step.

That sentiment crosses all ages, races, creeds, and other categories. I've had grandmothers caring for their children's children because the parent is incapable or unwilling. I've had retired African-American veterans who served this country for most of their lives. My riders have also included successful people in business who are worried about the workforce. Young people are evaluating the worth of a college education.

Almost all of them need a strong and vibrant nation to succeed. I also believe the way to success is freedom. Freedom to win, freedom to fail, freedom to learn from failure, pick oneself up and try again.

Uber drivers in Mobile have the unique privilege of giving rides to merchant ship workers from all over. My experience is that at least 80-90 percent of them want a ride to one destination.

Walmart.

To them, there is no better representation of what it means to be American. We take for granted something many of them can't get back home. Our freedom and ingenuity give them a myriad of choices at affordable prices.

I still have faith in the ideals that made America great. The next time I get in my car, turn on my Uber app, and begin giving rides, I'll meet people from all over the world, including all over America. Our citizens and others worldwide need the United

States of America to thrive again. I have hope!

We may have our flaws, but I believe strongly in this quote from Ronald Reagan:

"It's said that prayer can move mountains. Well, it's certainly moved the hearts and minds of Americans in their times of trial and helped them to achieve a society that, for all its imperfections, is still the envy of the world and the last, best hope of mankind."

"THE TREE WHY'S, MEN!"

Or Women, for that matter. In most conversations, we have concerns about who, what, and how. At least, that's my experience in my sixty-seven years of life. We don't learn much about someone unless we ask, "Why?"

I thought about this recently when I picked up a couple on their way to the Mobile Airport. The gentleman was gregarious, which is a considerable understatement.

He asked me if I had ever watched the cooking shows on Fox10.

"No," I told him, "I'm usually working or driving around those times."

"Well," he said, "I have a cooking show and do demonstrations at places like Rouses. I go by the name Chef Nino!"

That gave me the who and what. But Chef Nino was just beginning to exhibit his enthusiasm. "I love what I do and want other folks to love what they're doing. That's why I'm writing this book!" (1st Why!)

He continued, "I've already got the title and several supporters. They're all helping get this whole thing started. They're going to help me get interviews all over the country. I can produce the number of copies I need for each trip instead of printing a massive number and then trying to sell all of them." (Well, there are some of the Hows.)

"What's the name of your book?" I asked.

"That's the thing I like the most! The title is, *How To Create a Circus!*"

(Here it comes.) "Why that title?" I asked.

"Because life is crazy most of the time. You have to cause a stir to make things happen. You can't do things the way they've always been done. It's a circus!"

He went on, "I want to do more than teach people how to cook. I want them to learn how to be excited about living their lives. I want to travel all over and help people learn how to cope with everything in their lives! That's why I want to be a speaker: to thank God for all He's given me!"

The 3rd Why.

Once you get to the 3rd 'Why,' you can learn most of what you need to know about someone. This is true whether the person is a new acquaintance or a loved one.

As parents, many of us have resorted to the response, "Because I said so!" when asked "Why?" too many times. I know I have.

I think about many of my riders. You don't always have to say 'Why?' to get the answer. You have to listen carefully, and you'll often hear it.

I think about the young drug addict I picked up last year. He explained to me that he was going to rehab the following day for the third time. He was dreading the detox time that he would again have to endure.

"My family and my friends are disgusted with me." (1st 'Why?')

"I'm disgusted with myself and the life I'm living." (2nd 'Why?')

"I want to have a life. I want to raise a family. I want to make my family and friends believe in me. I want to be the father and husband that I should be someday. I don't think I can wait any longer to start that life." (Yes, those reasons are the 3rd 'Why?')

I could go on and on about my conversations with riders, friends, or family members, but you get the point. Sometimes, though, the conversations with myself that go on in my head are the ones that continue to ask the 'Why?' question. Those can be the most helpful.

A good friend once told me that my blogs sometimes sound a little preachy. Well, let me tell you why. I wrote these columns not to preach but to learn. That's why I'm always so grateful to have weekly conversations with my readers of the blogs. I always appreciate the feedback, even the ones with which I disagree. I'd like to thank all my readers for taking their time!

Maybe in a future story (adapted from a blog, of course), I'll give you a 3rd 'Why?' Stay tuned.

"DADS & FOOTBALL!"

It was almost Bama football season! I know there are other teams, but this time of year always made me think of my dad. He was a huge Alabama fan. He passed away 17 years ago on August 25, 2006. My mom left our lives on December 15, 2003.

Football season, especially Alabama football, nourished many conversations between my dad and me. The post-game phone calls when I was in college and all the years afterward were very special for us.

Fatherhood would be on my mind a lot then. I belong to a group called 'The Men of St. Joseph.' We aim to '*put the family back in the hands of the Father.*' It's a challenge to us as fathers, but more importantly, a duty to God the Father.

We held our yearly weekend retreat at the Visitation Monastery two weeks before this happened. Father Joseph Mary Wolfe, of EWTN fame, spoke to us about St. Joseph, his fatherhood, and other topics dealing with heart and soul. Forty men, almost all of them dads, listened intently to his message.

That week, I picked up a young man, similar to so many others I've picked up Ubering. He told me that he was going to his girlfriend's house. He asked about me. I told him I'd been married for forty-two years, and we had five children, all married to good people, and six grandchildren, with two more on the way.

"I'm a father, too," he said. "You got any advice for me?"

From his conversation, I knew he wasn't on the way to the mother of his child. "How old is your daughter?" I asked.

"She's about nine months old," he said.

I gave him some tips and let him know that the best way to learn is to be around to correct the many mistakes you'll make while learning to be a father. I'm still learning. I know my son and sons-in-law have to learn, but I'm enjoying watching them, teamed with wonderful wives and mothers. (They're way ahead of me!)

He seemed grateful as we ended the ride, but I worried he wouldn't get the complete picture. Marry a great woman, and your chances increase significantly. Stay with a good woman, and they increase geometrically.

I've thought a lot about the women riders I've picked up, along with too many children they're trying to raise alone. I can't count the number of times a grandmother raised these children because neither parent was responsible enough to be there.

I could go on about the challenges I've seen for these fatherless families, but that's for another story on another day. (I've covered that in past "political" columns.)

Alabama plays Middle Tennessee State in the opening game a week from Saturday. I'll be watching, and I'll be thinking about my dad. I'll think about how sports, especially college football, bring families and friends together, even when we don't always cheer for the same team. I'll also be thinking about how blessed I am to have the family I have.

* * *

I wrote a story recently about a world traveler I've Ubered several times. After I wrote that story and published it as a blog post, I picked him up again. (Luckily, he doesn't read my blogs. It could have been an awkward ride!)

We talked about his upcoming trip to Europe. Again, it was early in the day, and I picked him up at a bar. He told me his relationship with his dad was strained and how much he wished it wasn't. He asked me about my family. Big mistake! It takes a relatively long ride to cover the joy my family gives me and how proud I am of them.

I paused because I could see he was affected by what I said.

As he sat next to me in the front passenger seat, slapping his thighs with both hands, I could see he was holding back tears.

"What's wrong?" I asked. "Are you ok?"

When he regained his composure, he said, "There is one thing I've never had, and I never will. I've always wanted to be a dad to a daughter. No matter what else I do, I will always have that regret."

We finished the drive to his parent's house in silence. As he left the car, he looked at me and said, "You have no idea how lucky you are. I hope you never forget that."

Alabama will kick off in eleven days. I'll be watching. I'll be thinking about my dad and grateful that my good friends in the Men of St. Joseph remind me to put the '*family back in the hands of the Father!*' I'll also never forget how blessed I am to have a beautiful family and wonderful friends.

I hope the very same for you! And, 'Roll Tide!'

"FOUR SEASONS!"

I attended my high school's 50th Reunion celebration last weekend. We all enjoyed renewing acquaintances and updating our life stories from these last five decades. This particular story is not about the reunion, but the event caused me to contemplate the seasons of our lives we now experience.

When most people consider the seasons of their lives, spring is the first quarter, followed by summer, fall, and winter. Based on actuarial tables, I suppose most of my classmates fall into the fallish-winterish periods of life. I think about this often as I pick up my Uber passengers.

I love to think about where they are in their seasons. It's only sometimes age-related.

For example, a couple of weeks ago, I picked up a doctor heading for Mobile's Regional Airport. He was flying back to Raleigh, NC, after seeing a patient here in Mobile. He was originally from Ecuador.

"Why are you seeing a patient in Mobile?" I asked.

"I work for a company that uses technology developed in Germany to treat stroke patients," he explained. "Most Americans are treated with very outdated technology that consists of cheap plastic pieces.

"I recently took classes to update myself on stroke rehabilitation and realized the technology was no different from what educators taught me twenty-five years ago. The equipment my company is trying to use in the United States has a proven track record of successful and complete rehabilitation of stroke victims."

"So, what's stopping the use in this country?" I asked.

The frustration was evident in his voice. "Only the wealthy can use our technology. The insurance coding system has thrown obstacle after obstacle in our way. We're not cheap, but we're very, very effective."

As we neared the airport, he regained his enthusiasm. "It may take us a while, but there has to be a way to get approval for something that actually works but costs more versus a system that rarely gives the patient complete use of their arms and legs but is cheaper. The gap between the cost and the amount they can charge a patient is more profitable."

I hope he is successful. He certainly was passionate!

* * *

Later that day, I picked up a young lady from the Maritime Training Center on Battleship Causeway. She told me she was taking a welding course at the center.

"Most other jobs for women my age in this area are limited to nursing, teaching, and other jobs I'm either not interested in or trained for," she explained. "I believe I can make good money welding, or so I've been told. Right now, my biggest challenge is math. I was never good at math in school. I had no idea there would be this much math in welding."

One of my favorite recent podcasts was a discussion between Mike Rowe (with the mikeroweWORKS Foundation and of 'Dirty Jobs' fame) and Dave Ramsey, a radio personality and personal financial advisor to millions. My rider would benefit significantly from their advice on that show. Mike Rowe has featured a very successful woman welder/mechanic on a few of his podcasts.

I couldn't help becoming enthusiastic about my rider's potential as she pursued this career. As for her concern about math skills, we discussed everything from adult introductory education courses offered locally to multiple online courses. She preferred in-person training, and while I didn't know a specific option, we discussed several possibilities.

She promised to pursue the additional math classes and listen to Mike Rowe and Dave Ramsey. I made her write those down so she wouldn't just forget. We were both fired up by the end of the ride. I hope her enthusiasm didn't fade! After all, she vowed to her Uber driver, and there is almost no higher commitment!

* * *

Soon after, I picked up a very young lady who expressed a desire to become a writer. We focused on blog writing. I promised to help her in any way possible, gave her my email address, and asked her to send her posts when she started.

So, you can imagine my thrill when she sent me an email the next day!

Whitney wrote,

'Dear Mr. Tommy,

It was a pleasure seeing you yesterday. I look forward to talking to you and learning valuable information about starting my blog. I am attaching my first blog post, entitled "Carpe Diem."'

I read Whitney's blog, which I thoroughly enjoyed, and gave her a few suggestions.

She wrote back to me:

'Thank you so much, Mr. Tommy. I will implement your suggestions. I already have my second blog idea in the works. I appreciate your kindness and encouragement!!!'

What I've written above can seem very self-serving. It is. It may be the season I've reached in my life. I want to take the lessons from my many mistakes and use them to help others. I am still learning from others, older and younger than me, and I will for the remaining seasons of my life.

With my first rider above, I saw his determination and hope drive his desire to help as many stroke victims as possible. The second rider wanted to find a way to be more than others expected of her. She was willing to face the uncomfortable present challenges for a future of accomplishment. And my third rider dared to accept help from a new source. I didn't take advantage of that in my younger life nearly enough.

I loved the stories I heard from my classmates at our fiftieth reunion. We may be close to the same age, but we're not always in the same season of our lives. One of the things I love about Ubering is the opportunity to discover where in their life's seasons they're living. I still have so much to learn!

"A–MAZE!"

My wife and I spent last weekend with our oldest two daughters and their families. We don't get to spend nearly enough time with our kids and grandkids. Sweet Season Farms in nearby Milton, Florida, provided a great family venue for our time together.

We slid on slides, fired corn cobs from some kind of mortar gun, enjoyed a hayride, rode a cow train, and ate carnival food! But, my favorite part of the day was walking through the "Reba McEntire" Country Music Corn Maze.

Our group of nine ranged in age from 67 to our five-year granddaughter. Our 16-year-old granddaughter and 15-year-old grandson rounded out the 3rd generation of our team.

The key to successfully navigating the twists and turns depended on two 'clue' quizzes. One quiz asked random questions about Reba, while the other focused on corn trivia. We felt good about our venture until we reached clue #5. Not only did we miss the questions from each category, which told us whether to take a left or right turn, but there were several lefts or rights. We tried all of them.

We found the #5 clue sign at least a half dozen times. We sighed and said, "At least we only have six clues to get ourselves outta here!"

Then, one of our 'clue-holders' informed us that there were ten clues. Thank goodness no one in our family curses (out loud)!

Time for a new strategy! Most of our group would remain stationary. Our 'scouts' took each path, staying within earshot, and reported whether they reached a dead end or returned to the group after circling back to home base. At least one was successful in finding a continuing path.

So many unproductive circles and dead-end travels! But, to use a seasonally appropriate phrase, '*The halftime adjustments were the keys to our victory!'*

What a team accomplishment!

* * *

That Sunday afternoon, I picked up a lady for Uber. She had been through a rough couple of days, slept late, and wanted to relax and enjoy a mid-afternoon meal that she didn't have to cook. When we arrived at the family-owned soul food diner, it was closed. I already had another ride on the app but offered to take her to any alternative. She was so worried that she was inconveniencing me.

"Take your time," I said, "If the ride cancels, I'll get a new one."

She was still a little nervous but finally gave me the address of another restaurant. We had only gone a mile toward that one when she spotted another diner we had passed. I made a quick U-turn and delivered her. She was so apologetic but relieved. Several dead ends, unproductive circles, and final success!

See what I mean?

* * *

My last ride on Sunday afternoon was another example. Unfortunately, this was not the only time I've experienced this scenario.

After waiting past the 'cancel' time, I waited to pick up two young guys. One kept texting me that he was on his way but never seemed to move. After the app gave them the 'last chance' message, they hustled to the car.

We were heading toward one of the more unsavory inns on the Beltline service road. This motel had earned its terrible reputation. Unfortunately, I'd seen quite a mix of kids and folks down on their luck—combined with individuals who you might compare to some of San Francisco's contemporary citizens.

The guys in my car counted cash in the back seat while

slurring unintelligible conversation. Their odor gave evidence of their 'state of mind.' I drove by slowly until they saw the room number they wanted.

Remember the maze? These guys were stuck in a dead end. I've seen enough of this to recognize they might never get a clue and, except for a few unproductive circles, might never reach daylight. Sad.

* * *

Finally, I picked up a single mother of two small children after a couple of days. I was driving her to the U-Haul place after hours because she was to pick up a truck. Her landlord had given her two days to move out of her rental house.

"I complained to him about the air conditioner. After days of asking for relief, he sent some guys out with instructions to do just enough to keep it running for a few days. Then, the landlord told me the other company was charging more than $800.00. The problem is that I heard the contractor tell him it would be $440.00.

"My sister can let us stay for one week with her, but I'll have to go to a hotel after that. That's why I have to put our furniture in storage. But I told my kids that God will take care of us. I'm still going to feed them and get them to school."

"And" she continued, "God did take care of us! I found out today that we qualify for Section 8, and after a period of paperwork, we'll be able to start looking for a place to live on our own! God has always shown up for us! I broke down in tears when I saw the letter saying we qualified."

It seemed to me that she reached out to angels in her maze. They checked out the paths, eliminated the useless circles and dead ends, and gave her a course to safety. As I said, we've all got mazes, and we all have angels.

Here's another surprise. When I got home later that night, my phone dinged. That familiar tone told me someone had given me a tip. With all her troubles, my evicted single mother took the time to consider me.

The world can be so good sometimes! Keep on praying!

"FIVE PERCENT!"

I mentioned last week that my favorite holiday of the year is Thanksgiving! This one was one of the best! My wife and I welcomed our 8th grandchild into the world. I can't wait until our first in-person visit! We returned a few weeks ago from meeting our 7th in Chevy Chase, Maryland. We spent the holiday weekend with four grandkids and expect to see the other two in early January.

I'm so grateful. That's why some of my Uber riders sometimes mystify me. One of my rides last week exemplified the life of someone who might be missing the blessing of gratitude.

I picked her up at a local watering hole. She was sitting at an outdoor table with two other patrons. She already had her to-go box, so I figured she was ready to leave. She recognized my Uber sign, looked at me, and said, "I'll be right there." Except, she didn't make a move.

Several minutes later, she opened the back door and hopped in.

"How was your evening?" I asked.

"It was nice," she said. "Just spent some time with some friends of mine. How long have you been Ubering people? Are you retired and doing this to keep busy?"

"Nope. I have a full-time job during the day, but I drive on nights and weekends. It helps fill in the gaps, money-wise. I've given rides to more than 17,000 people for almost seven years. I've met some fantastic people and listened to some fascinating stories.

"I write a weekly blog. I've learned a lot from so many of my riders." I continued. "I've written about 130 stories."

"You should write a book! You could stop driving and make a fortune if you learn to promote yourself the right way.

You have to learn to be aggressive and not afraid to take no for an answer."

"Well, I have published a book before, so I do have a grasp of what I want to accomplish with my next one."

"Do you want to be a five or a ninety-five?" she challenged. "My dad used to ask me whether I wanted to be a five or a ninety-five! So, what is it for you?"

"Well, I'd like more context before I answer. Five stupid people or five winners? What's the context?" I asked. I know where she's going, but I feel like challenging her a little.

"Winners! Successful! Rich!! That's what the five stands for! So, five or ninety-five?" She was getting fired up now.

"Well, five would be better than ninety-five in that context. Now, let me ask you something. What is your definition of winner, or successful, or for that matter, rich? I've had money before. I've been a successful businessman, except when I wasn't. I've had more than my share of wins and losses."

"You need to hire an agent. Get the right agent, write your book, submit it to all the big publishers, promote it, and prepare to get turned down dozens and dozens of times before you get it published. If you're not aggressive, you'll never reach happiness!" she insisted.

Now she'd reached into my area. "I work during the day for the Little Sisters of the Poor. Every morning, I go to a place that cares for what you might call the '95'. I get to ask for help from thousands of people from the '5' and '95', and they give. All levels of people contribute."

I continued, "I've never been happier in my life. I have a wonderful wife, five 'successful' children and their spouses, and eight beautiful grandchildren. My goal is to make enough money to travel and visit those grandchildren. I have that plan, and I'm well on the way to achieving it!"

I then asked her, "What makes you happy in your five

percent life?"

"I've been successful!" she said. "I built a company to a $100 billion venture! I know success. But then, the other people disagreed with my direction, and we parted ways. I lost everything! I spent the next several months living under the bed. I suffered from severe depression.

"I'm working my way out of it now! It's put a toll on my family. My son and I have parted ways. My daughter and I are still together. But I can replicate the model and build another company from scratch. I can get that money back again," she insisted.

"What is it about the money that you depend on for happiness?" I asked.

"I could give that money to charities like yours. I'd still get what I want, but think how much good I could do if I were that rich! You should write and sell that book the way I told you."

I thought about that. I don't think we were on the same page. I've heard that line of thought often. I will believe it when I know that the individual is giving from what they have now, not what they will provide later.

"I'd like to give you a copy of my book. I'd also like to ask you to read my blogs. You said you wanted to know more about me. That would be the best way," I said.

"I will read your blogs. I promise. I appreciate the book, but I don't have any cash with me. I should pay you for your book."

"Most people just add it to the tip. You can do that if you wish."

"That's perfect! I'll do it!" she promised.

We finally reached her house.

So, there is one thing I hear from my fellow Uber drivers. If a rider tells you they will tip you on the app, ninety percent of the time, they don't. Tips usually come unannounced. I'm assuming this rider will tip me immediately after her next billion. I'm patient.

In the meantime, I want to thank my family, friends, co-workers, and the people I come into contact with daily! You are my five percent, and I mean that in the best way possible. You make me happy!

I've asked for prayers for the underdogs in the past. Please keep the 'winners' in your prayers. I think she needs them, too.

"THE CANDLES!"

I visit a tiny chapel every Monday morning from 6:00 am until 7:00 am. For several years now, at least one person has been in there, spending an hour of quiet time. Maybe some other time, I'll get more into the details of those visits, but here, I want to talk about the candles.

On each side of the altar in that chapel, there are twenty-four candles, twelve in a row, two candles deep. These candles are designed to last approximately five days. At various times, visitors make small donations and light a candle. Some will run out of wick very soon, and some are just beginning.

I look at the candles and try to decide which represents my life span and the ratio of the life I've lived to the life that's remaining. I think about all the people who have affected my life. I think about the lives of people I've met through ridesharing with Uber and Lyft.

I picked up an elderly lady at a grocery store a few weeks ago. As we approached her home, she told me that she had no family but needed help with repairs to her house. She asked me to drive to the back of her home to unload her groceries.

"You see what's happening up there, don't you?" she asked. "The wood is rotting away, and I don't have the money to fix it. I'm scared it will rot away." There was someone who could help her. I gave her a name.

* * *

Several months after that, I picked up a grisly old man from a bar. He spent a lot of his time in bars talking about his time as a veteran. He shared some of that with me.

"We got along with each other in the military," he said. "We had something in common and saw the world's worst and best. It wasn't like that when we got back. I spent almost twenty years in prison for a bar fight. The other guy died."

He was still alive, but his candle was reaching the end. He admitted it was mostly his fault, but he'd wasted most of his life. There were people who could help this man get some of his life back.

I've given rides to several people doing everything possible to extend the useful life of their candles.

* * *

When I picked her up, she was about two doors down from the address I was given. She had a suitcase.

"I guess you know what's going on here," she said.

I didn't.

"I'm leaving my husband for good. I've made mistakes picking men throughout my life. I'm giving up guys until I've raised my daughter. I owe her my full attention."

I believed she was serious. I hoped her commitment to her daughter was long-term. She was responsible for her candle as well as her daughter's. There was someone who could help her.

While so many of my memorable rides include conversations with people down on their luck, so many others have been uplifting. Mobile has hosted lots of conventions, conferences, and seminars for groups dedicated to solving many of the challenges I've mentioned in this column. Really good people!

When I look at those candles in the chapel, I'm perfectly aware that it only takes a tiny wisp of wind to extinguish the light, regardless of the length of the wick.

So, here's where I'm going with this. During the life of my candle, I've seen people go through horrific experiences. Some have survived, rarely without help, but most needed assistance.

The beautiful thing about our community is that countless folks are willing to help. They need the means to turn intentions into actions.

Well, this is the season. During these next few weeks, Catholic Churches in South Alabama will ask their parishioners to give a portion of their blessings to help their fellow citizens. These donations will fund 30 charities, including my own Little Sisters of the Poor.

Last year, donors contributed more than $5,000,000.00 to help aid the poor, home repairs, charitable pharmacy services, emergency assistance, youth groups, prison ministries, education, hospital ministries, crisis pregnancy services, adoptions, and so much more.

The vast majority of help goes out to non-Catholics. Even more important, donations are vastly multiplied by the thousands of volunteers who help those in need. You don't have to be Catholic to contribute.

I think about those candles I see every Monday morning. I think about the light given off by the flames. I've been in so many communities that need our help. We can lift those in need out of their darkness. I hope you'll help!

"WE, THE PEOPLE!"

No matter what anyone tells you, there is an 'I' in *people*. And there is an 'I' in *team*. But if you look for the 'I' in *America*, it's not where you think. There is no 'We the People' without 'I.'

William F. Buckley, Jr. once said, "I believe that everyone is different from everyone else in every conceivable way."

I'll take that one step further. I believe I'm dramatically different from what I was twenty years ago. I think no one on earth is exactly like me or anyone else like you.

Society says that polite folks don't engage in conversation with strangers about politics or religion. I guess my riders and I have violated that rule more times than I can count. So inevitably, our discussion revolves around the theme of most of my chapters. '*What Do We Really Want?*'

A while back, I picked up a young lady from Goodwill Industries. She entered my car with a huge bag.

"I had to buy some clothes for my husband to wear to a funeral." She explained, through tears, that her family was vacationing along the Emerald Coast when two of the kids got caught in a riptide. Her sister-in-law struggled to rescue the children, along with her sister-in-law's husband, who was able to pull one of them to shore. The mother struggled to stay afloat and pushed her husband toward the other child. He saved the second child. Sadly, his wife passed away.

My rider cried as she tried to understand why God would do this to their family. Even though her faith was strong, she could not find the words to help her husband through this— dealing with the loss of his sister. We all have human emotions, even with dramatically different life experiences. She had my prayers.

* * *

That same night, I picked up a truck driver at a restaurant

to take him to a truck stop. We joked around about how long we would live. I showed him an app that counts how many days until I am 100. He said he would like to go back thirty years to re-live his early twenties. He felt that he had made several mistakes that he would correct. Our conversation lasted several minutes after our ride ended. We touched on life experience, faith, and even a little politics.

* * *

Afterward, I picked up a 'fifty-something' year-old man who had just finished working overtime for his employer. He brought up our current political travails. He said, "I'm getting so tired of being told what I think and what my limits are by people who don't even know me."

He told me his family and friends felt the same way but were scared to say it aloud. "I tell everyone: *I decide who I am, nobody else!*"

* * *

Later, I picked up a repeat customer for the third time. She came to Mobile less than a year ago. She came from a fractured childhood and was now raising her son alone. He was out of town, and she was concerned that he hadn't made any friends yet at his high school. They came from a rough neighborhood in New York, and she had hoped to create a new life for them in Mobile. Unfortunately, the pandemic prevented the natural formation of friendships during his first year at a new school in a new town. He hadn't made those connections even now.

So, what was the point? All these folks desired relationships with people around them. Each case started with a personal decision to reach out to someone else. It means risking our vulnerability. We start one-to-one. The 'I' in each of us reaches out.

You may notice that I never mentioned the race or nationality of any of those riders. It doesn't make any difference. Each of these people can change their lives by

242

individual initiative. Likewise, one person can change the lives of others.

* * *

A few years ago, my wife and I enjoyed attending Cooper Riverside Park's 4th of July celebration. We sat in our lawn chairs right next to Mobile River, along with thousands of folks there to celebrate our country's independence. I noticed no divisions by race or color, only a mixture of people enjoying patriotic music and fireworks.

Some children were sitting near us with their respective families. Some were white, and some were black. A very young white girl was attempting to play catch with her brother as they unsuccessfully tried to toss a beach ball to each other. A little black boy hopped up and joined the game, helping the brother and sister retrieve the beach ball. A couple of other very young children joined in. I 'saw' that they were of different colors. I 'noticed' and cherished that it made no difference to them. They soon played with other 'toss and catch' toys, laughing and running together.

I hope nobody takes the time to point out their surface differences as they grow up. It's not just kids. You see it every time we have major storms like hurricanes and tornadoes. Truthfully, living in downtown Mobile, we saw it every day. People reach out to others.

Uber allowed me to visit with people from around the world. On that 4th of July, I couldn't help but realize that although all of us are different, we have so much in common. I hope this chapter doesn't come across as preaching. My riders have convinced me that we can reach out to one another as individuals with varying needs and desires.

We the People' is a worthy concept, and it starts with realizing that the 'I's' have it within our grasp.

God Bless America!

"SO MANY EXPERTS!"

We all do it, don't we? Each one of us believes we're experts on something. I know a few people who think they're experts on everything. I'm pretty sure I've landed between the something and the everything category at one time or another.

As an Uber driver and life-liver, I've often offered my expert testimony. And I have indeed received wisdom from among my 18,000 riders.

There was the New York visitor who lectured me about the backward lifestyle of the Deep South. He started with landmarks in Mobile, including the George Wallace Twin Tunnels. "We would never tolerate that sort of affront in New York!" he exclaimed.

We had a lively discussion for the next thirty minutes. He remained in my car for about fifteen minutes after we reached his destination. To my passenger's credit, he softened his criticism after he listened to the story of Wallace's support from the very community he had once opposed.

"Well, maybe Alabama has come a long way, but you're still backward! I'll have to think about the things you've said." He was somewhat less sure of his expertise.

* * *

Several times, I picked up the father of a local high school football player. Sports and politics provide more 'experts' than any other source I can imagine.

Each time I picked up this dad, he spent the entire ride on the phone with someone. I didn't have to struggle to listen to the conversation. You know the type I'm talking about. Their whisper is louder than most folk's yell!

"That @%#$ coach has no idea what he's doing. Most of the parents support him because they don't want him to be mad at them! I'm not that type! I've watched enough football in my life to know what he's doing wrong."

I don't know whether he was right or wrong. I know this guy's attitude would make it difficult for him to convince anyone.

Years ago, my wife and I had season tickets to Alabama's home football games. We reluctantly gave them up so we could be with our children as they participated in various high school sports and other programs. By the way, we've never regretted that decision.

We signed up again for season tickets when they had completed their high school years. We had to start over at the bottom of the ladder, and after a year's wait, we got two tickets in the corner of the stadium. If you've been to Bryant-Denny Stadium, you would recognize that the most talked-about feature is the ability to be one of the last folks to stare into the blazing sun until sunset.

There are a lot of experts who sit up there. But, without a doubt, one 'gentleman' was substantially more vocal than anyone else. He described precisely why the coach's call was idiotic in graphic detail. I've always been amazed that the powers that be would assign the worst seats to one of our top coaching advisors. Besides, I'm not sure Nick Saban or any other coach could hear this guy's wisdom. But we love our sports and politics precisely because we can be experts without being judged by the consequences of our advice in action.

I'm a baby boomer. I tell you that so you know how long I've been on this planet. I work in an atmosphere that includes another generation senior to mine. I consider those older folks experts in their lives and experiences. But I also know that I have the opportunity to learn something from everyone I meet, of any age.

* * *

I've Ubered veterans of many generations who have told the stories of their lives. Expert stories. I have listened to single

245

mothers who have found ways to raise children through sacrifice and hardship. I have heard former convicts testify about how they turned their lives around after taking personal responsibility for their situations.

We have all heard from other experts about how different people or 'society' caused their problems. Countless people will validate those opinions for them.

I got an Uber call to pick up an older gentleman one afternoon. He was a veteran who had gotten into trouble one night after spending too much time in a bar. He got into a fight and ended up killing another man over a stupid argument.

He sounded like 'Red' in *Shawshank Redemption.* "I wish I could go back and talk to that young man," he said. "I wish I could change what I did way back then. I was drunk and stupid. The world changed a lot during the time I spent in prison."

He continued to tell me that he would try to talk to young men today who he saw traveling the same path he chose. He believed some of them listened. After all, he was an expert.

We have more access to wisdom and knowledge than ever before. I spend a lot of time in my car listening to podcasts on various subjects. I will not live long enough to learn everything I want to know.

Even after hearing all the experts, I know I must ultimately apply the expertise to my life. That's the only thing I can specialize in. Too many of us look to experts for the perfect answer. I'm learning to listen for *an* answer, not just *the* answer.

"DRIVE—BY MEMORIES!"

Sometimes, it's about people, and sometimes, it's about places. After almost eight years and more than 8,300 rides as an Uber driver, I've revisited my life journey hundreds of times. I've spent most of my time here on earth in Mobile, Alabama, and its nearby communities. So many memories!

For example, every time I drive through the Brookley Complex, I recall the stories my parents told me about my birth at Brookley Air Force Hospital. My dad was an air traffic controller in the U. S. Air Force, stationed far away from Mobile.

My mom's doctor guesstimated my arrival for late October 1955. My dad subsequently obtained a two-week leave of absence to be present for my birth. Of course, doctors were not always as accurate as those in the present. So, he got another two weeks. But again, in air traffic controller jargon, I was neither on course nor on glide path.

So, he pled for an additional three days. Still, no baby. The military allowed one more day. Nope. That was it. He had used every option, even borrowing as far into the near future as possible.

On November 28, 1955, I decided I was ready to enter the outside world, just a few hundred yards from Mobile Bay. But we eventually met when Dad managed to accrue enough off-time. He never seemed to hold it against me, even as my parents retold the story over the years.

My Uber travels took me through neighborhoods that included memories of my times at my grandparents' homes. My father's parents lived on Charles Street, just a few streets from the old Malbis Bakery on South Broad Street. Our family lived two doors from 'Big Daddy' and 'Big Mama.' One of my earliest memories is sitting on my grandparents' porch, drinking milk left on their front porch by the milkman.

My mom's parents, 'Grandpa' and 'Nanny,' lived in a more upscale neighborhood on McDonald Avenue, north of Ladd Stadium. My memories included a 'rumpus' room on the first floor of the two-story home. They had two kitchens, one upstairs and one downstairs. They also had a separate apartment in the backyard.

One of the more unique features was a bathroom that opened to the backyard, intended for the hired help who worked in their yard. I guess that was a compromise to accommodate folks who would otherwise not be allowed inside to visit the 'facilities.'

Each year, their house hosted Senior Bowl parties, intended initially to schmooze the top customers of their family business, which they founded on Mardi Gras Day in downtown Mobile in 1933.

That brings up another memory. The company my grandparents founded was eventually located on Telegraph Road just south of the Chickasaw line. I started working at Finch Warehousing and Transfer Co., Inc. at fourteen. After graduating from the University of Alabama with a degree in Transportation, I spent much of my life working at the family business.

Our family no longer has a business there. That story is too long to cover here. I published a book in 2009 that chronicles a portion of my time there. It's called *An Act of Congress, the Real-Life Story of Power and Politics in Family Business.* But that's not the subject of this story.

My Uber rides often take me within the vicinity of our warehousing business. Most of my memories of my time in that area are very positive. My passengers never leave from that area, nor do they arrive nearby. I sometimes drive by the buildings just to reminisce about the challenges and, mostly, the victories during my time there. More than anything else, I think about the wonderful people who affected my life while I was there.

Time has changed the places I've spent much of my life. I think about the people who affected my life and are tied to the places I drive. I miss them. Friends, co-workers, clients and customers, vendors, and just plain folks fill my memories as I drive through.

I drive through neighborhoods that remind me of childhood friends, school teachers, neighbors, coaches, and people I've had the privilege to know. Fourth grade at St. Pius Catholic Grade School around Sage Avenue. Football and baseball teams at Sage Park. Fifth through eighth grade at St. Dominic with the Sisters of Mercy, who taught us much more than reading, writing, and arithmetic.

I spent my high school years at McGill Institute during its final year as an all-boys high school. We studied across the street from the all-girls Bishop Toolen High School. Besides studying the fairer sex, we had actual subjects taught by the Brothers of the Sacred Heart.

Each time I pass these places, I conjure up warm memories of the people I grew up with and around. During part of my adult life, I sold residential and commercial real estate in the same territories where I now transport ride-share passengers to their destinations. My various careers, volunteer opportunities, political involvement, and life experiences have taken me to every nook and cranny of my hometown.

I will retire soon from the Little Sisters of the Poor, a 'place' that is as human and loving as anywhere I've been.

I drive by where my wife and I raised our children and built memories. These drives remind me of their growth and the challenges they've overcome. No matter where I spend the rest of my life, my home will always be the streets, corners, parks, and buildings in Mobile, Alabama.

I stated in the first paragraph, "Sometimes, it's about people, and sometimes it's about places." But the truth is that I never drive by a place without thinking about the people who've affected my life. I'm grateful for those places and those people.

"A VERY NEW YEAR! HAPPY?"

One day, I picked up a family on Ft. Walton Beach. A mom, two of her sons, and a daughter tossed their bags in the rear of my VW Tiguan. One of the boys carefully placed his fishing rod on top of the other luggage. The mom sat up front with me.

Uber instructed me to take the family to the Destin/Fort Walton Beach airport.

"Where are y'all from?" I asked.

"We came from Chicago," she answered. "See the middle one back there? We flew down here Thursday after Christmas to celebrate his birthday. Today was the first good weather day, so we practically had to drag him from the pier.

"My husband and one other son had to stay in Chicago. This was our first trip to the Florida panhandle, but we will definitely return."

I asked the birthday boy, "Did you have any luck fishing?"

"Yep. I caught fish every day, even in the rain. Fish don't care," he said.

His mom and I continued our conversation. She discussed the possibility that she and her husband would love to retire in this area, but they were still a decade away from that decision.

"You never know where the kids and their families will settle. We have the same challenges as our parents. My parents wanted warmer climates, so they moved to San Diego. My dad passed away, so my mom moved closer to us."

Her conversation made me think about all our 'life decisions' each year. 2024 was a pivotal year for me. Retirement. But not really. I never planned to stop working, not that it is financially viable.

If I were honest, I do have goals or 'resolutions' for 2025. I want to write, and I want to speak to audiences. As an Alabama football fan, I've learned the importance of 'process,' as demonstrated by Coach Nick Saban.

So, here is my plan:

1. **Practice gratitude:** Despite the challenges we face as humans, my life has been filled with blessings, more than I can count. I've met people worldwide and had the opportunity to see good and bad. My challenges have been tough, but I've seen so much worse. My sources of gratitude are my family, friends, and the people with whom I've had the privilege of knowing.

2. **Awareness:** Sixty-nine is a weird age. In some circles, my last job at Little Sisters of the Poor, for example, I feel more like 'middle-aged.' But in most cases, I've reached an age of discernment. So, at the end of each day, I'll revisit the times when I moved toward or away from the person I want to be. What did I learn?

3. **Messages:** Did something happen that was meant to steer me in a particular direction? I'm still driving for Uber. Whether through conversations or observations, am I learning something that is supposed to define my pathway?

4. **Others:** If you have been a long-time reader of my blogs, or even if you've come this far reading, you know I've often expressed the need to pray for my riders and others needing help. I hope I never let a day go by that I don't ask God to intercede.

I didn't invent this plan. I keep a card in my wallet and on my desk. Matthew Kelly and his colleagues at Dynamic Catholic distribute these cards worldwide. My 'process' came from them. I've copied it below:

THE PRAYER PROCESS

1. **GRATITUDE:** Begin by thanking God in a personal dialogue for whatever you are most grateful for today.

2. **AWARENESS:** Revisit the times in the past twenty-four hours when you were and were not the best version of yourself. Talk to God about these situations and what you learned from them.

3. **SIGNIFICANT MOMENTS:** Identify something you experienced in the last twenty-four hours and explore what God might be trying to say to you through that event (or person).

4. **PEACE:** Ask God to forgive you for any wrong you have committed (against yourself, another person, or Him) and to fill you with a deep and abiding peace.

5. **FREEDOM:** Speak with God about how He is inviting you to change your life so that you can experience the freedom to be the best version of yourself.

6. **OTHERS:** Lift up to God anyone you feel called to pray for today, asking God to bless and guide them.

7. **PRAY:** The Our Father.

I have so much more to learn. If I have one singular resolution, it is to continue my life education using the knowledge my family and friends share with me. My mother and one of my best friends passed away at the age of sixty-nine. I am nowhere near the person they were. Thanks for sharing your time with me. You continue to bless me with your support.

My title says, *'A Very New Year! Happy?'* I hope and pray that your 2025 is successful and very **HAPPY!**

EPILOGUE

"IT'S IN THE AURA!"

More than 9,000 trips as a ride-share driver. I started driving because I wanted my new (used) car to pay its own way. That's occurred in spades! I had no way of knowing how many ways my life would be affected by my passengers.

I've hesitated to tell this story because I don't want anyone to think what I've experienced is unique to me. It's not. The following examples are just a few, but I think you'll get the flavor. I've told most of these stories before, but I'd like to add more detail, especially during this unique time.

Right after I began driving, I picked up a group of folks from a restaurant passing through Mobile on their way to Dallas to visit a close relative. They knew this would be their last chance to see him before cancer would take him away. We shared a conversation about how short life can seem and the importance of making an impact while we're on this earth.

We stayed in the car well after I had reached their hotel destination. We talked about how small things can bother us so easily. Their vehicle had two flats at the same time, which is why they used an Uber to go to dinner. That was the first time I heard the phrase.

"There's an aura in this car."

We all agreed that our conversation had lifted everyone's spirits, including mine.

"There's a reason we had those flat tires. We needed this time and these words," they said.

* * *

Over the years, I've had dozens of riders tell me that there was something in the air in my car. Many used other descriptions, but several specifically used the word 'aura.'

Most of them just needed someone to whom they could talk. On two occasions, my riders were contemplating suicide.

255

Other times, the riders were fighting addictions, marital challenges, family dysfunctions, and other life experiences.

Lest you think I'm even pretending to be an expert in any of those fields, let me assure you I'm most assuredly not. I'm not even a particularly good listener. (The last sentence describes a life goal! My wife will tell me when I've reached that pinnacle.)

Why am I bringing up all of these stories now? Maybe it's the events of last weekend and a need to change the discussion tone.

* * *

One last story. This one is a little personal; I've only shared it with a few people.

I picked up a young family at a trampoline facility on Airport Blvd. The father, mother, and young son were going to a hotel on the other side of the airport. If you've ever tried to walk across, you know you're taking your life in your hands.

All three sat in the back seat. They had trouble securing the little boy, so I helped him get buckled up. We didn't talk much on the short trip. When we reached their hotel, the woman told the other two to get out quickly.

"I need to tell our driver something."

She breathlessly continued, "As soon as I got in your car, I felt a pressure on my chest. Suddenly, I knew I was supposed to tell you something. I could feel an 'aura,' and God wanted me to tell you this!

"He says to let you know you're doing exactly what you are supposed to be doing at the exact time you should be doing it! I have no idea why I'm supposed to tell you that or what it means. He also says he has big plans for your future. Does this mean anything to you?" she asked.

It did. For days, I wondered why I was spending so much

time driving other folks around. Was this the best use of my time?

I don't know what plans God has for me, but as of this moment, I have received no calls asking me to be the vice president, so it must be something different.

ABOUT THE AUTHOR

Tommy Fulton has given rides to more than 18,000 riders in the last eight years. His passengers have shared countless stories, many times in intimate detail. Tommy's life experiences as a family man, business owner, civic and charitable group leader, and personal challenges give him a unique perspective on life challenges.

Tommy Fulton has ridden life's roller coaster, and those ups and downs have given him an empathetic ear. Somehow, many of his riders perceive that openness. This book tells many of their stories.